The Crusades: A Very Short Introduction

VERY SHORT INTRODUCTIONS are for anyone wanting a stimulating and accessible way in to a new subject. They are written by experts, and have been published in more than 25 languages worldwide.

The series began in 1995, and now represents a wide variety of topics in history, philosophy, religion, science, and the humanities. Over the next few years it will grow to a library of around 200 volumes – a Very Short Introduction to everything from ancient Egypt and Indian philosophy to conceptual art and cosmology.

Very Short Introductions available now:

ANARCHISM  Colin Ward
ANCIENT EGYPT  Ian Shaw
ANCIENT PHILOSOPHY
  Julia Annas
ANCIENT WARFARE
  Harry Sidebottom
THE ANGLO-SAXON AGE
  John Blair
ANIMAL RIGHTS  David DeGrazia
ARCHAEOLOGY  Paul Bahn
ARCHITECTURE
  Andrew Ballantyne
ARISTOTLE  Jonathan Barnes
ART HISTORY  Dana Arnold
ART THEORY  Cynthia Freeland
THE HISTORY OF
  ASTRONOMY  Michael Hoskin
ATHEISM  Julian Baggini
AUGUSTINE  Henry Chadwick
BARTHES  Jonathan Culler
THE BIBLE  John Riches
BRITISH POLITICS
  Anthony Wright
BUDDHA  Michael Carrithers
BUDDHISM  Damien Keown
BUDDHIST ETHICS  Damien Keown
CAPITALISM  James Fulcher
THE CELTS  Barry Cunliffe
CHOICE THEORY
  Michael Allingham
CHRISTIAN ART  Beth Williamson

CHRISTIANITY  Linda Woodhead
CLASSICS  Mary Beard and
  John Henderson
CLAUSEWITZ  Michael Howard
THE COLD WAR  Robert McMahon
CONSCIOUSNESS  Susan Blackmore
CONTINENTAL PHILOSOPHY
  Simon Critchley
COSMOLOGY  Peter Coles
THE CRUSADES
  Christopher Tyerman
CRYPTOGRAPHY
  Fred Piper and Sean Murphy
DADA AND SURREALISM
  David Hopkins
DARWIN  Jonathan Howard
DEMOCRACY  Bernard Crick
DESCARTES  Tom Sorell
DESIGN  John Heskett
DINOSAURS  David Norman
DREAMING  J. Allan Hobson
DRUGS  Leslie Iversen
THE EARTH  Martin Redfern
EGYPTIAN MYTH
  Geraldine Pinch
EIGHTEENTH-CENTURY
  BRITAIN  Paul Langford
THE ELEMENTS  Philip Ball
EMOTION  Dylan Evans
EMPIRE  Stephen Howe
ENGELS  Terrell Carver

ETHICS  Simon Blackburn

THE EUROPEAN UNION
  John Pinder

EVOLUTION
  Brian and Deborah Charlesworth

FASCISM  Kevin Passmore

FEMINISM  Margaret Walters

FOSSILS  Keith Thomson

FOUCAULT  Gary Gutting

THE FRENCH REVOLUTION
  William Doyle

FREE WILL  Thomas Pink

FREUD  Anthony Storr

GALILEO  Stillman Drake

GANDHI  Bhikhu Parekh

GLOBALIZATION
  Manfred Steger

GLOBAL WARMING  Mark Maslin

HABERMAS
  James Gordon Finlayson

HEGEL  Peter Singer

HEIDEGGER  Michael Inwood

HIEROGLYPHS  Penelope Wilson

HINDUISM  Kim Knott

HISTORY  John H. Arnold

HOBBES  Richard Tuck

HUME  A. J. Ayer

IDEOLOGY  Michael Freeden

INDIAN PHILOSOPHY
  Sue Hamilton

INTELLIGENCE  Ian J. Deary

ISLAM  Malise Ruthven

JOURNALISM  Ian Hargreaves

JUDAISM  Norman Solomon

JUNG  Anthony Stevens

KAFKA  Ritchie Robertson

KANT  Roger Scruton

KIERKEGAARD  Patrick Gardiner

THE KORAN  Michael Cook

LINGUISTICS  Peter Matthews

LITERARY THEORY
  Jonathan Culler

LOCKE  John Dunn

LOGIC  Graham Priest

MACHIAVELLI  Quentin Skinner

THE MARQUIS DE SADE
  John Phillips

MARX  Peter Singer

MATHEMATICS  Timothy Gowers

MEDICAL ETHICS  Tony Hope

MEDIEVAL BRITAIN
  John Gillingham and Ralph A. Griffiths

MODERN ART  David Cottington

MODERN IRELAND  Senia Pašeta

MOLECULES  Philip Ball

MUSIC  Nicholas Cook

MYTH  Robert A. Segal

NATIONALISM  Steven Grosby

NIETZSCHE  Michael Tanner

NINETEENTH-CENTURY
  BRITAIN  Christopher Harvie and
  H. C. G. Matthew

NORTHERN IRELAND
  Marc Mulholland

PARTICLE PHYSICS  Frank Close

PAUL  E. P. Sanders

PHILOSOPHY  Edward Craig

PHILOSOPHY OF SCIENCE
  Samir Okasha

PLATO  Julia Annas

POLITICS  Kenneth Minogue

POLITICAL PHILOSOPHY
  David Miller

POSTCOLONIALISM
  Robert Young

POSTMODERNISM
  Christopher Butler

POSTSTRUCTURALISM
  Catherine Belsey

PREHISTORY  Chris Gosden

PRESOCRATIC PHILOSOPHY
  Catherine Osborne

PSYCHOLOGY  Gillian Butler and
  Freda McManus

QUANTUM THEORY
  John Polkinghorne

RENAISSANCE ART
  Geraldine A. Johnson
ROMAN BRITAIN   Peter Salway
ROUSSEAU   Robert Wokler
RUSSELL   A. C. Grayling
RUSSIAN LITERATURE
  Catriona Kelly
THE RUSSIAN REVOLUTION
  S. A. Smith
SCHIZOPHRENIA
  Chris Frith and Eve Johnstone
SCHOPENHAUER
  Christopher Janaway
SHAKESPEARE
  Germaine Greer
SIKHISM   Eleanor Nesbitt
SOCIAL AND CULTURAL
  ANTHROPOLOGY
  John Monaghan and Peter Just
SOCIALISM   Michael Newman

SOCIOLOGY   Steve Bruce
SOCRATES   C. C. W. Taylor
THE SPANISH CIVIL WAR
  Helen Graham
SPINOZA   Roger Scruton
STUART BRITAIN   John Morrill
TERRORISM   Charles Townshend
THEOLOGY   David F. Ford
THE HISTORY OF TIME
  Leofranc Holford-Strevens
TRAGEDY   Adrian Poole
THE TUDORS   John Guy
TWENTIETH-CENTURY
  BRITAIN   Kenneth O. Morgan
THE VIKINGS   Julian Richards
WITTGENSTEIN   A. C. Grayling
WORLD MUSIC   Philip Bohlman
THE WORLD TRADE
  ORGANIZATION
  Amrita Narlikar

Available soon:

AFRICAN HISTORY   John Parker
  and Richard Rathbone
ANGLICANISM   Mark Chapman
THE BRAIN   Michael O'Shea
CHAOS   Leonard Smith
CITIZENSHIP   Richard Bellamy
CONTEMPORARY ART
  Julian Stallabrass
THE DEAD SEA SCROLLS
  Timothy Lim
DERRIDA   Simon Glendinning
ECONOMICS   Partha Dasgupta
THE END OF THE WORLD
  Bill McGuire
EXISTENTIALISM   Thomas Flynn
THE FIRST WORLD WAR
  Michael Howard
FUNDAMENTALISM
  Malise Ruthven

HIV/AIDS   Alan Whiteside
INTERNATIONAL RELATIONS
  Paul Wilkinson
JAZZ   Brian Morton
MANDELA   Tom Lodge
THE MIND   Martin Davies
PERCEPTION   Richard Gregory
PHILOSOPHY OF LAW
  Raymond Wacks
PHILOSOPHY OF RELIGION
  Jack Copeland and Diane Proudfoot
PHOTOGRAPHY   Steve Edwards
PSYCHIATRY   Tom Burns
RACISM   Ali Rattansi
THE RAJ   Denis Judd
THE RENAISSANCE   Jerry Brotton
THE ROMAN EMPIRE
  Christopher Kelly
ROMANTICISM   Duncan Wu

For more information visit our web site
www.oup.co.uk/vsi/

Christopher Tyerman

# THE CRUSADES

## A Very Short Introduction

OXFORD
UNIVERSITY PRESS

# OXFORD

UNIVERSITY PRESS

Great Clarendon Street, Oxford OX2 6DP

Oxford University Press is a department of the University of Oxford.
It furthers the University's objective of excellence in research, scholarship,
and education by publishing worldwide in

Oxford New York

Auckland Cape Town Dar es Salaam Hong Kong Karachi
Kuala Lumpur Madrid Melbourne Mexico City Nairobi
New Delhi Shanghai Taipei Toronto

With offices in

Argentina Austria Brazil Chile Czech Republic France Greece
Guatemala Hungary Italy Japan Poland Portugal Singapore
South Korea Switzerland Thailand Turkey Ukraine Vietnam

Oxford is a registered trade mark of Oxford University Press
in the UK and in certain other countries

Published in the United States
by Oxford University Press Inc., New York

British Library Cataloguing in Publication Data

Data available

Library of Congress Cataloging in Publication Data

Data available

ISBN 13: 978-0-19-280655-0
ISBN 10: 0-19-280655-6

7 9 10 8

Typeset by RefineCatch Ltd, Bungay, Suffolk
Printed in Great Britain by
Ashford Colour Press Ltd, Gosport, Hampshire

*For*

P. P. A. B.

# Contents

Preface   xi

List of maps   xiii

List of illustrations   xiv

Introduction   1

1   Definition   12

2   Crusades in the eastern Mediterranean   19

3   Crusades in the west   42

4   The impact of the Crusades   53

5   Holy war   64

6   The business of the cross   86

7   Holy lands   109

Conclusion   136

Further reading   145

Chronology   148

Index   154

# Preface

While the 18th-century Scottish philosopher and historian David Hume thought the Crusades 'the most signal and most durable monument of human folly that has yet appeared in any age or nation', he admitted they 'engrossed the attention of Europe and have ever since engrossed the curiosity of mankind'. The reasons for this are not hard to find. The twin themes of judgement on past violence and fascination with its causes have ensured the survival of the Crusades as more than an inert subject for antiquarians. Since Pope Urban II (1088–99) in 1095 answered a call for military help from the Byzantine emperor Alexius I Comnenus (1081–1118), by summoning a vast army to fight in the name of God to liberate eastern Christianity and recover the Holy City of Jerusalem, there have been few periods when the consequences of this act have not gripped minds and imaginations, primarily in western society but increasingly, since the 19th century, among communities that have seen themselves as heirs to the victims of this form of religious violence. With the history of the Crusades, modern interest is compounded by spurious topicality and inescapable familiarity. Ideological warfare and the pathology of acceptable communal violence are embedded in the historical experience of civilization. Justification for war and killing for a noble cause never cease to find modern manifestations. The Crusades present a phenomenon so dramatic and extreme in aspiration and execution and yet so rebarbative to modern sensibilities, that they cannot fail to move both as a story and as an expression of a society remote in time and attitudes yet apparently so abundantly recognizable. Spread over five hundred years and across three continents, the Crusades may not have defined medieval Christian Europe, yet they provide a most extraordinary feature that retains the power to excite, appal, and disturb. They remain one of the great subjects of European history. What follows is an attempt to explain why.

The phenomenon of violence justified by religious faith has ebbed and flowed, sometimes nearing the centre, sometimes retreating to the margins of historical and contemporary consciousness. When I was asked to write this short introduction to the Crusades, holy war, Christian or otherwise, was not high on the public or political agenda. Now when I have finished, it is. So this work conforms to a pattern traced in what follows, of historical study relating to current events. My views on that relationship will, I hope, become clear enough. What remain hidden except to the lynx-eyed are the debts to many other scholars, colleagues, and friends from whom I have learnt so much and should have remembered so much more. They must forgive a collective thanks. The faults in this *libellus* are mine not theirs. The dedication is a very small recompense for incalculable munificence of advice, support, and friendship over so many years, in dark days as well as bright evenings of exhausting but inexhaustible hospitality.

C. J. T.

Oxford

22 May 2005

# List of maps

A.  Medieval Europe and its frontiers   20
B.  Europe and the Mediterranean: Christianity and its
    non-Christian neighbours   24
C.  The Near East in the 12th century   27
D.  The Crusader states of Outremer   28
E.  The Spanish Reconquista   46
F.  The Baltic   49
G.  The Aegean in the 13th and 14th centuries   55
H.  The castles of Outremer   112

# List of illustrations

1   Richard I as crusader   4
Illustration by John Kenney from
*Richard the Lionheart* by L. du
Garde Peach. © Ladybird Books
Ltd, 1965, reproduced by
permission of Ladybird Books
Ltd.

2   Saladin and Richard I   5
Illustration by John Kenney from
*Richard the Lionheart* by L. du
Garde Peach. © Ladybird Books
Ltd, 1965, reproduced by
permission of Ladybird Books
Ltd.

3   President Assad's Saladin,
    Damascus 1992   6
© Benno Graziani/Photo12.com

4   Richard I and Jerusalem,
    1917   11
© Punch Ltd

5   Urban II in 1095   13
Bibliothèque nationale de France,
Paris (MS Lat. 17716 fol. 9 recto).
Photo: © Bibliothèque nationale
de France

6   Fifteenth-century
    drawing of the Edicule of
    the Holy Sepulchre   15
Badische Landesbibliothek,
Karlsruhe (St Peter pap. 32,
fol. 45 verso). Photo: © Badische
Landesbibliothek

7   Pilgrim returning from
    Jerusalem – P. Michel,
    *Les Fresques de Travant*
    (Paris 1944)   17
By permission of the British
Library (LR 430 n 9, pl. XIX)

8   The loss of the relic of the
    True Cross at the battle
    of Hattin, 1187   31
Corpus Christi College,
Cambridge (MS 26, p. 279). By
permission of the Master and
Fellows of Corpus Christi College

9   Frederick Barbarossa as
    crusader   33
Biblioteca Apostolica Vaticana
(MS Vat Lat 2001 fol 1 recto).
Photo: Biblioteca Apostolica
Vaticana

10   Twelfth-century plan of the Church of the Holy Sepulchre   35
Österreichische Nationalbibliothek, Vienna (NB 24376). Photo: © Österreichische Nationalbibliothek

11   Muslim Christian warfare in Spain – *Candigas de Santa Maria*, Monastery of Escurial, Madrid   48
Institut Amatller d'Art Hispanic, Barcelona. Photo: © Arxiu Mas

12   A medieval world map   54
By permission of the British Library (MS Roy 14C IX fol. 1)

13   Mamluks at military exercises   60
By permission of the British Library (Add MS 18866, fol. 8140)

14   Thirteenth-century English crusader knight   84
By permission of the British Library (MS Royal 2A XXII, fol. 220)

15   Bernard of Clairvaux at Vézelay – by E. Signol, 1838   87
Musée national du Château de Versailles, France. Photo: © ARJ/Photo12.com

16   Embarking on Crusade   95
Bibliothèque nationale de France, Paris (MS fr. 4274, fol. 6). Photo: © Bibliothèque nationale de France

17   Crac des Chevaliers   114
© Jane Taylor/Sonia Halliday Photographs

18   Jerusalem   119
Koninklijke Bibliotheek, The Hague (MS 76 F5 fol. I recto). Photo: © Koninklijke Bibliotheek

19   Saint James fighting the Moors, attrib. Circle of Juan de Flandes   123
Museo Lázaro Galdiano, Madrid. Photo: © Museo Lázaro Galdiano

20   Louis IX at Damietta   133
Bibliothèque nationale de France, Paris (MS fr. 2628, fol. 328). Photo: © Bibliothèque nationale de France

21   Cook's Crusader 1898   141
© Punch Ltd

22   Saladin and Saddam Hussein – Iraqi propaganda, 1980s   143
© Sipa Press/Rex Features

The publisher and the author apologize for any errors or omissions in the above list. If contacted they will be pleased to rectify these at the earliest opportunity.

# Introduction

Between 1189 and 1191, a cosmopolitan army of western invaders besieged the Palestinian coastal city of Acre, modern Akko. Their camp resembled the trenches of the Western Front during the First World War, fetid, disease-ridden, and dangerous. One story circulated to boost morale concerned the heroic death in battle a few years earlier of a knight from Touraine in France, Jakelin de Mailly. A member of the Military Order of Knights Templar, a soldier who had taken religious vows of poverty, chastity, and obedience in order to devote his life to protecting Christians and their conquests in Syria and Palestine, Jakelin had been killed fighting a Muslim raiding party in Galilee on 1 May 1187. In describing what proved to be a massacre of the Christians, the story had Jakelin fighting on alone, hopelessly outnumbered and surrounded. The chronicler who recorded the story before 1192, possibly an Englishman and certainly a veteran of the siege of Acre, is worth quoting in full:

> He was not afraid to die for Christ. At long last, crushed rather than conquered by spears, stones and lances, he sank to the ground and joyfully passed to heaven with the martyr's crown, triumphant. It was indeed a gentle death with no place for sorrow, when one man's sword had constructed such a great crown for himself from the crowd laid all around him. Death is sweet when the victor lies encircled by the impious people he has slain with his victorious right hand . . . The place where he fought was covered with the stubble

which the reapers had left standing when they had cut the grain shortly before. Such a great number of Turks had rushed in to attack, and this one man had fought for so long against so many battalions, that the field in which they stood was completely reduced to dust and there was not a trace of the crop to be seen. It is said that there were some who sprinkled the body of the dead man with dust and placed dust on their heads, believing that they would draw courage from the contact. In fact, rumour has it that one person was moved with more fervour than the rest. He cut off the man's genitals, and kept them safe for begetting children so that even when dead the man's members – if such a thing were possible – would produce an heir with courage as great as his.

Except possibly for the suggestion of sexual fetishism, this story, which would not have convinced all who heard it by any means, represented a standard piece of crusade propaganda. Crusading, fighting for God in return for a promise of salvation, placed a premium on courage, physical prowess, martial skill, and religious conviction. As such, little separated it from other forms of organized violence. Yet the tale of Jakelin de Mailly emphasized certain features particularly characteristic of the Crusades, especially the belief or assertion that violence for the faith will earn heavenly reward. The killer, already a professed religious, becomes a holy man, a martyr, a witness for his God. Such is the hero's spiritual potency that his physical remains retain a powerful material charge to confer his human qualities to others, even posthumously through his sexual organs. His horrible, violent death was interpreted as 'gentle' and 'sweet'; his memory provided inspiration; his remains were thought to convey virtue. Death was a completion but no conclusion.

On the face of it, few mentalities – enthusiastic for violence, fixed on an afterlife – could be less accessible to modern observers in the western cultural tradition than this. Yet no aspect of Christian medieval history enjoys clearer modern recognition than the Crusades, nor has been more subject to egregious distortion. Most of what passes in public as knowledge of the Crusades is either misleading or false. The Crusades were not solely wars against Islam in Palestine. They were not chiefly conducted by land-hungry younger sons, nor were they part of some early attempt to impose western economic hegemony on the world. More fundamentally, they did not represent an aberration from Christian teaching. Nonetheless, interest and invention exist as two sides of the same historical coin. That in part explains why the world of Jakelin de Mailly and his eulogist has not been consigned to the same obscurity as that of medieval scholastics or flagellants; that and the drama of the events themselves. Jakelin's death in a desperate and foolhardy skirmish in the Galilean hills may arouse only modest interest. But his presence two thousand miles from his homeland; the cause for which he swore religious vows, fought, and died; the region for which he battled; and the memorable historical figures drawn into the conflict in which he served have ensured his endeavour and sacrifice can still touch a nerve. That is the excuse for this book.

The word 'crusade', a non-medieval Franco-Spanish hybrid only popularized in English since the 18th century, has entered the Anglo-American language as a synonym for a good cause vigorously pursued, from pacific Christian evangelism to militant temperance. However floridly and misleadingly romantic, the image of mailed knights bearing crosses on surcoats and banners, fighting for their faith under an alien sun, occupies a familiar niche in the façade of modern western perceptions of the past. Despite, or perhaps because of, its lack of context, it remains the indelible image of crusading in popular culture, shared even by the sculptors of the late President Assad of Syria. Iconography is never innocent. Assad's Damascus Saladin is defeating the Christians at their own imperialist game as surely as the Ladybird's Saladin and Richard I are playing out some 19th-century cultural minuet. Polemicists and politicians know – or should know – that to invoke the Crusades is to stir deep cultural myths, assumptions, and prejudices, a fact recognized by Pope John Paul II's apology to Jews, Muslims, and

1. Richard I as a romantic warrior hero, depicted in the children's Ladybird History *Richard the Lionheart* (1965). The contrast between the imposing figure of Richard and the semi-clad 'native' opponents speaks of a marriage between lingering 19th-century imperialism and stock fabrications of popular neo-medievalism.

2. Eastern sophistication confronts western brute force. In this fictional encounter, from the Ladybird *Richard the Lionheart*, Richard I has broken an iron bar with his great sword while Saladin's delicately sharp scimitar cuts a silk handkerchief. This typology traces its ancestry to Gibbon in the 18th century and beyond.

3. Saladin as a modern Islamic hero. The statue shows Saladin as victor of Hattin, with an infantryman and a sufi – sword and faith. It was commissioned by the city of Damascus, Syria, in 1992.

Eastern Orthodox Christians for the intolerance and violence inflicted by Catholic warriors of the cross. Although it is difficult to see how even Christ's Vicar on earth can apologize for events in which he did not participate, over which he had no control, and for which he bore no responsibility, this intellectually muddled gesture acknowledged the continued inherent potency of crusading, a story that can still move, outrage, and inflame. One of the groups led by the fundamentalist religious terrorist Usama bin Laden was known as 'The World Islamic Front for Crusade against Jews and Crusaders'. To understand medieval crusading for itself and to explain its survival may be regarded as an urgent contemporary task, one for which historians must take responsibility. To this dual study of history and historiography, of the Crusades and what could be called their post-history, this is a brief introduction.

Casual modern acquaintance with the Crusades stems from the wide dissemination of crusading motifs from the early 19th century, a rather precious, sentimental vision of an invented medieval past, as in Walter Scott's popular and influential *Ivanhoe* and *The Talisman*, the latter actually set during the Third Crusade. A similar sentimentality infected continental responses; romantic images of crusaders became a stock in trade for artists and poets. The cultural familiarity on which the force of these works relied was maintained into the 20th and 21st centuries chiefly by the popular media of Hollywood, television, and imaginative literature, not all of it describing itself as fiction. Crossovers between history and entertainment at least suggest a market, if only for what the great American crusader scholar of the first half of the 20th century, J. La Monte, forensically described as 'worthless pseudo-historical trash'.

Crusading has left a physical imprint on Europe. Most obviously, impressive sites associated with crusading or the military orders remain, such as Aigues Mortes in the Rhone Delta, from where Louis IX of France embarked for Egypt in 1248, or the

14th-century headquarters of the Teutonic Knights at
Marienburg in Prussia (now Malbork in Poland). Some reminders
invoke a sombre message: the plaque at Clifford's Tower in York
commemorates the Jews who died there in March 1190, victims by
murder and suicide of Yorkshire crusaders. More intimate
evocation of personal responses and the strenuous conviction of
individuals thirty to fifty generations ago can be found in quiet
corners like the 11th-century church at Bosham, Hampshire, on the
edge of Chichester Harbour, whose great chancel arch saw Harold
Godwineson on his way across the Channel to a fateful meeting
with Duke William of Normandy in 1064 and earned a place in the
Bayeux Tapestry. Crosses etched deep in the stone of the door jambs
and a cross of Jerusalem more lightly scratched on a nearby pillar,
whether marks of anxious hope on departure or of thankful relief at
a safe return, speak directly of a physical ideal, witness in almost the
ultimate degree of devotion to a belief in the tangibility of the divine
that allowed ordinary, faithful laymen, through their own action
and the material relics of their God and His Saints, to touch
Paradise. That identical crosses can also be seen incised on the walls
of the Church of the Holy Sepulchre in Jerusalem emphasizes both
the startling reality of the experience of pilgrims and crusaders and
the gulf between their age and our own. Yet, such memorials leave a
trace in the mind.

Visible reminders are strewn across the modern landscape. In
London alone, without the Crusades there would be no shopping in
Knightsbridge, no cricket at St John's Wood, no law at the Temple –
all places that derive their names from the medieval landlords of
these suburbs, the Military Orders of the Temple and of the
Hospital of St John, religious orders originally established to
succour and protect pilgrims to Jerusalem in the aftermath of its
conquest by the first crusaders in 1099. Linguistic and material
survivals are matched by a more urgent and in some cases more
insidious recognition that has woven the memory of crusading into
some of the more intractable modern political problems, the Arab–
Israeli conflict, responses to Terrorism, religious inter-faith conflict,

the origins of western racism and anti-Semitism, and the nature of and reaction to European and American political and cultural imperialism.

Yet here lurks a paradox. The continuing popular and political resonance of crusading feeds on an historical phenomenon that, both in its own time and later, has lacked objective precision in definition, practice, perception, or approval. In the Middle Ages there existed no single word for what are now known as the Crusades. While those who took the cross were described as *crucesignati* – people (not exclusively male) signed with the cross – their activities tended to be described by analogy, euphemism, metaphor, or generality: *peregrinatio*, pilgrimage; *via* or *iter*, way or journey; *crux*, literally cross; *negotium*, business. This allowed for a flexibility of target and ideology that was matched by a concentration in canon law (the law of the church) on the behaviour of the crusader and the implications of the various privileges associated with the activity rather than any general theoretical formula specifically defining a legal concept of a crusade. Thus at the heart of this form of Christian warfare lay a possibly convenient ambiguity of ideas and action that spawned a wide diversity of responses. The wars of the cross, initiated to regain Jerusalem for Christianity in 1095 and extended over the next few generations to encompass a wide variety of violence against the Catholic Church's perceived external and internal foes, have been understood by participants, contemporaries, and later observers in a protean variety of ways.

By turns, crusading has been variously interpreted. It has been presented as warfare to defend a beleaguered Faith or the ultimate expression of secular piety. Alternatively, some have regarded it as a decisive ecclesiastical compromise with base secular habits; a defining commitment of the church to accommodate the spiritual aspirations of the laity. As the admired pinnacle of ambition for a ruling military elite, crusading is portrayed as an agent as well as symbol of religious, cultural, or ethnic identity or even superiority; a

9

vehicle for personal or communal aggrandizement, commercial expansion, or political conquest. More narrowly, the Crusades appear as an expression of the authority of the papacy in imposing order and uniformity within Christendom as well as securing its external frontiers. Conflicting assessments of the Crusades have described them as manifestations of religious love, by Christians for fellow believers and by God for His people; an experiment in European colonialism; an example of recrudescent western racism; an excuse and incentive for religious persecution, ethnic cleansing, and acts of barbarism; or a noble cause. Steven Runciman, the best-known and most influential anglophone Crusade historian of the 20th century, imperishably condemned the whole enterprise as 'one long act of intolerance in the name of God which is the sin against the Holy Ghost'.

Even shorn of present prejudices and preoccupations, the history of the Crusades throws up concerns central to all societies, from the forging of identities through the communal force of shared faith and the use and abuse of legitimate violence to the nature of political authority and organized religion. Crusading exemplifies the exploitation of the fear of what sociologists call 'the other', alien peoples or concepts ranged against which social groups can find or be given cohesion: Communism and Capitalism; Democracy and Fascism; Christians and non-Christians; Whites and Non-Whites; Them and Us. There can be no indifference to such issues. That is why the study of the Crusades possesses an importance beyond the confines of academic scholarship. Equally, there can be no summoning of the past to take sides in the present. Plundering history to deliver modern indictments serves no rational or benign purpose. To observe the past through the lens of the present invites delusion; so too does ignoring the existence of that lens. However, the burden of understanding lies on us to appreciate the world of the past, not on the past to provide ours with facile precedents or good stories, although of the latter the Crusades supply plenty.

## THE LAST CRUSADE.

CŒUR-DE-LION (*looking down on the Holy City*). "MY DREAM COMES TRUE!"

4. 'At last my dream comes true.' *Punch*'s response to the entry of General Allenby into Jerusalem in December 1917. Note the Union Jack flying over the Jaffa Gate to the left of the cartoon. In fact, Allenby carefully avoided any demonstration of overt imperialist or Christian triumph, making his entry on foot.

# Chapter 1
## Definition

At a council of the Church held at Clermont in the French Auvergne in November 1095 a decree was issued that marked a new beginning in western Christianity's use of war to further its religious mission.

> Whoever for devotion alone, not to gain honour or money, goes to Jerusalem to liberate the Church of God can substitute this journey for all penance.

This decree did not invent Christian violence. Nor did it define precise terms of a revolution in thought or practice, or determine how future generations would employ the precedent. Coming half way through a preaching tour of France conducted by Pope Urban II (1088–95), the Clermont assembly was best remembered not for the legal authority granted by the decree but for the pope's sermon at the end of the council on 27 November. What the pope said is not known. Witnesses and later commentators subsequently depicted him as delivering a rousing call to arms to the fighting classes of western Europe to recover the Holy City of Jerusalem, insisting that this was no ordinary act of temporal warfare but a task enjoined on the faithful by God Himself, a message echoed back in the cries of 'Deus lo volt!' – 'God wills it!' – said to have greeted Urban's words. To provide a focus for commitment and a sign of distinction, Urban instituted the ceremonial granting of crosses to those who had sworn to undertake the Jerusalem journey. Thus they became 'signed with the cross', *crucesignati*.

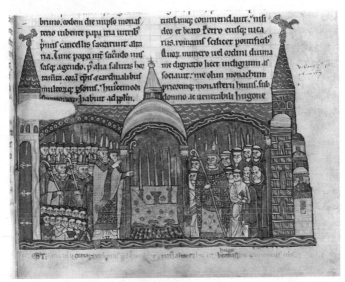

5. Urban II (on the left, his hand raised in blessing) consecrates the new church at his alma mater, the Burgundian abbey of Cluny, a month before he proclaimed the First Crusade at Clermont in 1095.

Over the following century writers in western European vernaculars began to describe these wars in similar terms – *crozeia, crozea,* or even *crozada* in early 13th-century southern French (*langue d'oc*). The appropriation of Christianity's most numinous symbol, as badge, banner, and talisman, followed naturally from the pope's conception of the enterprise to liberate 'the Holy City of Christ, embellished by his passion and resurrection'. Observers and veterans of the enterprise understood the pope to have called for Christ-like sacrifice in obedience to the gospel command: 'If any man will come after me, let him deny himself, and take up his cross, and follow me' (Matthew 16:24). All Hebrew accounts of the 1096 massacres of Rhineland Jews by the passing Christian armies emphasized that the butchers wore the sign of the cross.

The memory of Urban's rhetoric at Clermont played a central role in how the events prompted by his speech were later portrayed, providing a convenient start to narratives of the startling consequences of the pope's preaching. Urban's decree explicitly proclaimed a holy war in which the effort of the campaign, including the fighting and the inevitable slaughter, could be regarded as equivalent to strenuous performance of penance provided it had been undertaken devoutly. The cause may have been seen as just, but that was not the point. This was an act of total self-abnegating faith demanded by God, hence the language of unrealistic absolutes that failed to match military, social, and psychological reality, an ideal to inspire and against which deeds could be judged. The Clermont decree instituted a holy war, its cause and motive religious, an act of Christian charity for 'the love of God and their neighbour' (the eastern Christians). As well as combining violence with a transcendent moral imperative, Urban appealed to a form of 'primitive religious nostalgia' embodied in the ambiguously liminal Holy City of Jerusalem, lost to Christendom since its capture by the Muslims in 638 yet central to Christian imagination as the scene of the Crucifixion and Resurrection. Here, according to Christian texts familiar through the Mass and liturgy, earth touched heaven. In a short space, the Clermont decree identified reasons for the massive response: the certainties of faith; fear of damnation; temporal self-image; material, social, and supernatural profit; the attraction of warfare for a military aristocracy; an unequivocally good cause; and an iconic objective of loud resonance in the imaginative world of western Christians. It proved to be a formula of sustained power for the rest of the Middle Ages.

What we today call a crusade could be described as a war answering God's command, authorized by a legitimate authority, the pope, who, by virtue of the power seen as vested in him as Vicar of Christ, identified the war's object and offered to those who undertook it full remission of the penalties of confessed sins and a package of related temporal privileges, including church protection of family and

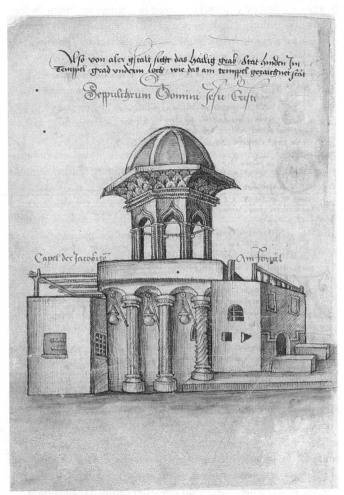

6. A 15th-century drawing by a German pilgrim of the Edicule (small house) built over the Holy Sepulchre within the Church of the Holy Sepulchre, the physical destination of so many pilgrims and crusaders over the previous four centuries.

property, immunity from law suits and interest repayments on debt. The beneficiary earned these grants by swearing a vow symbolized in a ritual adoption of a cross, blessed by a priest and worn on the recipient's clothing, the vow often being couched in terms parallel to those for a pilgrimage. The duration of the spiritual and temporal privileges was determined by the fulfilment of the vow, by absolution or by death. Those dying in battle or otherwise in fulfilment of their vow could expect eternal salvation and to be regarded as martyrs. At every stage, analogies with a quasi-monastic commitment were drawn, associating the activity with what remained the ideal conception of the perfect Christian spiritual life. Although details of the operation of the vow and its associated privileges developed over the following century or more to cover a multiplicity of political and ecclesiastical concerns, the first appearance and original justification for such a holy war in 1095 was the recovery of Jerusalem from Muslim rule. Thereafter, the Holy Land retained a primacy in rhetoric, imagination, and, for many centuries, ideology.

## Numbering the crusades

Historians organize the past to help them make sense of the evidence. In doing so they run the risk of becoming imprisoned by their own artifice. Between 1095 and, say, 1500 there were scores of military operations that attracted the privileges associated with the wars of the cross. Yet only a few later became known by a number, all of them aimed at Muslim targets in and around Syria and Palestine in the eastern Mediterranean. Obviously, the nobles, knights, foot soldiers, unarmed pilgrims, and hangers-on who answered Urban II's appeal in 1095-6 did not know they were embarking on the first of anything; they were told their efforts were in a unique cause. Subsequent events altered perceptions. The promoters of the next comparable eastern campaign, in 1146-9, invoked the precedent of 1095-6, casting into shadow smaller expeditions that had embarked to aid the Christian cause in the east in the interim. Thus, in the eyes of later scholars, the 1146 crusade

7. The crusade as a penitential exercise was intimately linked to the practice of pilgrimage. Here, in a wall-painting from St Nicholas Church, Travant, France, a 12th-century pilgrim is shown returning from Jerusalem bearing a palm leaf as evidence of the completion of his journey. Palm leaves could be bought in the Street of Palms in the Holy City.

became the Second Crusade. Subsequent numbering followed suit, attached only to general, large-scale international assaults intended to reach the Holy Land. Hence the inclusion in the canon of the Fourth Crusade (1202–4) that planned to attack Egypt, although getting no further than Constantinople. Other crusades are defined by objective, location, participants, or motive. Hence the Albigensian Crusades describe the wars against religious heretics in southern France around Albi between 1209 and 1229. The Baltic Crusades were campaigns launched against local pagan tribes of the region for two and a half centuries from the mid-12th century. The Peasants' (1096), Children's (1212), and Shepherds' (1251, 1320) Crusades speak for themselves, socially pigeon-holed by historians' (and contemporary) snobbery. The wars directed from the 13th century against papal enemies in Europe are called, somewhat judgementally, 'Political', as if all crusades, like all wars, were not political. The dozens of lesser crusades to the Holy Land not deemed large or glamorous enough have remained unnumbered. To add to the confusion, even within the canon, historians have disagreed over some numbers attached to Holy Land crusades in the 13th century. Some see Frederick II of Germany's crusade of 1228–9 that briefly restored Jerusalem as the Sixth Crusade; others as the last campaign of the Fifth Crusade summoned in 1213. Louis IX of France's Egyptian campaign of 1248–50 (the Sixth or Seventh depending on the view taken of Frederick II) and his campaign to Tunis in 1270 (the Eighth or Ninth) are not now generally described by number. Such games are not new. In the early 18th century some historians stuck to five (1096, 1146, 1190, 1217–29, and 1248) while others counted eight. Most modern historians, content to number crusades until the Fifth (beginning in 1213), thereafter dispense with numbering.

# Chapter 2
# Crusades in the eastern Mediterranean

## The First Crusade, 1095–9

Between 1095 and the end of the Middle Ages, western Europeans fought or planned wars broadly understood as being in defence or promotion of their religion throughout the eastern Mediterranean, in the Iberian peninsula, the Baltic, and within Christendom itself. Yet no campaign rivalled the first in impact or memory. Contemporaries and subsequent generations have been astonished and moved by the exploits of the armies and fleets from western Europe that forced their way into the Near East between 1096 and 1099 to capture Jerusalem in distant Palestine. Excited western intellectuals employed the language of theology: for one, 'the greatest miracle since the Resurrection'; for another, 'a new way of salvation', almost a renewal of God's covenant with His people.

The expedition arose out of a specific social, religious, ecclesiastical, and political context. Western Europe was held together by a military aristocracy whose power rested on control of local resources by force and inheritance as much as by civil law. The availability of large numbers of arms bearers, nobles and their retinues, with sufficient funds or patronage to undertake such an expedition, was matched by an awareness of the sinfulness of their customary activities and a desire for penance. For them, holy violence was familiar and Jerusalem possessed overwhelming numinous resonance. The invitation from the eastern Christian

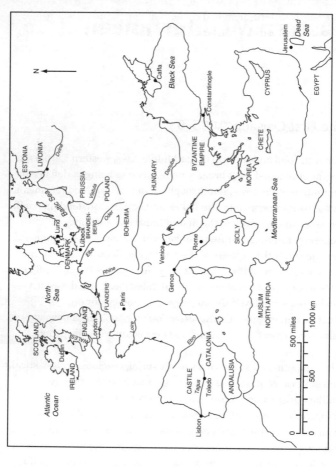

A. Medieval Europe and its frontiers

emperor of Byzantium (Constantinople), Alexius I Comnenus to Pope Urban suited the new papal policy of asserting supremacy over both Church and State developed over the previous half century. An earlier scheme by Pope Gregory VII (1073–85) to lead an army eastwards to Jerusalem had come to nothing in 1074. This time, Urban II, already a sponsor of war against the Muslims in Spain, seized on the opportunity to promote papal authority in temporal affairs. From its inception, crusading represented a practical expression of papal ideology, leadership, and power.

The opportunity was no accident. Alexius I had been recruiting western knights and mercenaries for years. A usurper, he needed military success to shore up his domestic position. The death in 1092 of Malik Shah, Turkish sultan of Baghdad, was followed by the disintegration of his empire in Syria, Palestine, and Iraq. This offered Alexius a chance to restore Byzantine control over Asia Minor and northern Syria lost to the Turks since their victory over the Byzantines at Manzikert in 1071. For this he needed western troops. For political convenience the pope was an obvious and ready ally to choose. Once he had received the Byzantine ambassadors early in 1095, Urban transformed their request for military aid into a campaign of religious revivalism, its justification couched in cosmological and eschatological terms. The pope himself led the recruitment drive with a preaching tour of his homeland, France, between August 1095 and September 1096 that reached its defining moment at Clermont. With the kings of France and Germany excommunicated, the king of England, William II Rufus, in dispute with the pope, and the Spanish monarchs preoccupied with their own Muslim frontier, the pope concentrated on the higher nobility, the dukes, counts, and lords, while casting his net wide. Recruitment stretched from southern Italy and Sicily to Lombardy, across great swathes of France from Aquitaine and Provence to Normandy, Flanders and into the Low Countries, western Germany, the Rhineland, the North Sea region, and Denmark, although both Latin and Arabic sources dubbed them collectively as 'Franks' – *Franci, al-ifranji*. A recent guess puts the number of fighting men reaching Asia Minor in 1096–7 at between 50,000 and 70,000, excluding the non-combatant pilgrims who used the military exodus as protection for their own journeys.

The first to set out for the agreed muster point of Constantinople in spring and summer 1096 included forces from Lombardy, northern and eastern France, the Rhineland, and southern Germany. One of their leaders was a charismatic Picard preacher known as Peter the Hermit. Some contemporaries attributed the genesis of the whole enterprise to Peter, who allegedly had been badly treated by the Turkish rulers of Jerusalem when on pilgrimage some years earlier. Although unlikely to have been the expedition's instigator, Peter certainly played a significant role in recruitment, possibly with papal approval, and was able to muster a substantial army within three and a half months of the council of Clermont. Elements of these Franco-German contingents conducted vicious anti-Jewish pogroms the length of the Rhineland in May and June 1096, before moving east down the Danube. Together, these armies have been dismissed as 'the Peasants' Crusade'. This is a misnomer. Although containing fewer nobles and mounted knights than the later armies, these forces were far from the rabbles of legend and contemporary polemic. They possessed cohesion, funds, and leadership, managing to complete the long march to Constantinople largely intact and in good time. One of the commanders, Walter Sans Avoir, was not, as many have assumed, 'Penniless' – Sans Avoir is a place (in the Seine valley), not a condition. However, discipline proved hard to maintain. After crossing the Bosporus into Asia in August 1096, these armies were annihilated by the Turks in September and October, only a matter of weeks before the first of the princely-led armies reached Constantinople.

Behind Peter's expeditionary forces came six large armies from northern France, Lorraine, Flanders, Normandy, Provence, and southern Italy. Although the Provençal leader, Count Raymond IV of Toulouse, had been consulted by Urban II in 1095–6 and travelled with the pope's representative, or legate, Adhemar, bishop of Le Puy, there was no single commander. The most effective field general proved to be Bohemund of Taranto, head of the Normans from southern Italy. Arriving at Constantinople between November 1096 and June 1097, each leader was persuaded or forced to offer an oath of fealty to Alexius I, who, in return, provided money, provisions, guides, and a regiment of troops. After the capture of Nicaea, capital of the Turkish sultanate of Rum (Asia Minor) in June 1097, the campaign fell into four distinct phases. An arduous march across Asia Minor to Syria (June to October 1097) that saw a major but close-run victory over the Turks north of Doryleaum (1 July) was followed by the siege and then defence of Antioch in northern Syria (October 1097 to June 1098). One contingent from the main army under Baldwin of Boulogne established control of the Armenian city of Edessa beyond the Euphrates. As their difficulties proliferated, the depleted western army increasingly regarded themselves as under the special care of God, a view reinforced by visions, the apparently miraculous discovery at Antioch of the Holy Lance that was said to have pierced Christ's side on the Cross, and the victory a few days later (28 June 1098) over a numerically much superior Muslim army from Mosul. From June 1098 until January 1099, the Christian army remained in northern Syria, living off the land and squabbling over the spoils.

The final march on Jerusalem (January to June 1099) was accompanied by reports of more miracles and visions, increasing the sense of the army being an instrument of Divine Providence. However, the crusaders may have been single-minded, pious, and brutal, but they were neither stupid nor ignorant. Their advance had taken account of local politics at every stage, notably the chronic divisions among their Muslim opponents that prevented united resistance. Amicable negotiations with the Egyptians, who had themselves conquered Jerusalem from the Turks in 1098, lasted for two years before collapsing only a few weeks before the westerners reached the Holy City. The final assault on Jerusalem (June to July 1099) was crowned with success on 15 July; the ensuing massacre shocked Muslim and Jewish opinion. Western

B. **Europe and the Mediterranean: Christianity and its non-Christian neighbours**

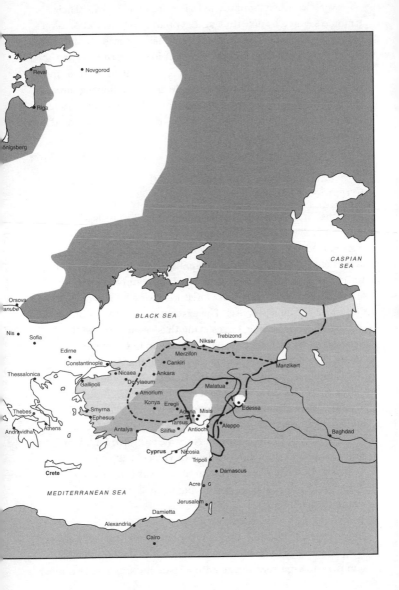

observers described it approvingly, in apocalyptic terms. Their triumph secured by defeating an Egyptian relief army at Ascalon (12 August), most of the surviving crusaders returned to the west. By 1100, as few as 300 knights were left in southern Palestine. Of the upwards of 100,000 who had left for Jerusalem in 1096, and of those who had caught up with them during the following three years, perhaps no more than 14,000 reached Jerusalem in June 1099. Urban II had been right: the war of the cross had proved a very severe penance indeed.

## The 12th century and the Second Crusade, 1145–9

After the First Crusade's establishment of bridgeheads at Antioch in Syria and Jerusalem in Palestine, four principalities were carved out on the Levantine mainland: the kingdom of Jerusalem (1099–1291); the principality of Antioch (1098–1268); the county of Edessa (1098–1144); and the county of Tripoli (1102–1289). Collectively these territories were known as Outremer, the land overseas. The eastern crusades were directed at expanding, defending, or restoring these conquests. In the first half of the 12th century, with Jerusalem in Christian hands, the pilgrim trade exploded, while campaigning in the Holy Land became part of chivalric training for some high-born nobles as well as a martial accessory to pilgrimage. A number of modest expeditions helped conquer the ports, plains, and immediate hinterland of the Syrio-Palestinian coast (for example, those of King Sigurd of Norway, 1109–10; Fulk V of Anjou, 1120 and 1128; and the doge of Venice, 1123–4). Increasingly, the model of penitential war was used on other Christian frontiers, such as Spain, and against papal enemies within Christendom.

However, the Holy Land retained its primacy as a goal of holy war. The precedent of the First Crusade ensured that a new general summons to arms received an enthusiastic response. In December

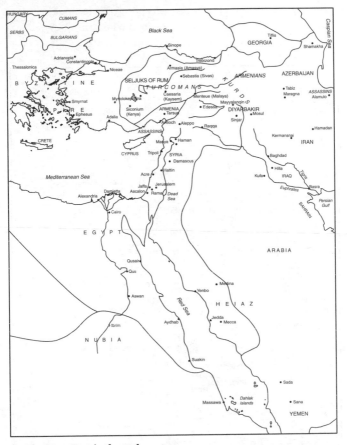

C. **The Near East in the 12th century**

1144, the Turkish warlord Zengi, ruler of Mosul and Aleppo
(1128–46), captured Edessa, massacring the Frankish inhabitants.
In response, Pope Eugenius III (1145–53) launched a fresh crusade
with a bull (that is, a circular letter, so called after its seal, or *bulla*)
that recited the heroics of 1096–9 as well as explaining the detailed
privileges available to those who took the cross. In contrast with
Urban II, Eugenius eagerly enrolled monarchs – Louis VII of

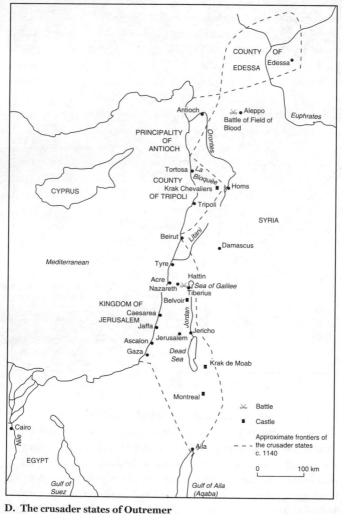

D. The crusader states of Outremer

28

France (1137–80) and Conrad III of Germany (1138–52). Recruiting lay chiefly in the hands of Abbot Bernard of Clairvaux (1090–1153), the dominant ecclesiastic and spiritual publicist of his generation who conducted a highly effective preaching tour of France, Flanders, and the Rhineland in 1146–7. Bernard's message of intolerance to Christ's enemies spilled over into more anti-Jewish violence in the Rhineland, although this was rather disingenuously blamed on a maverick monk called Rudolph. While the pope authorized separate crusading wars in Spain, Bernard allowed a group of disgruntled Saxon nobles to commute their Holy Land vows to fighting on the Baltic German/Slav frontier, which they did without conspicuous success or adherence to holy war in the summer of 1147. One substantial body of recruits from Frisia (a northeastern province of Germany, bordering the North Sea), the Rhineland, Flanders, northern France, and England, travelling east by sea, helped King Alfonso Henriques of Portugal (1139–85) capture Lisbon from the Moors (24 October 1147) after a brutal four-month siege. Some remained to settle, but most embarked for the Mediterranean the following spring, some finding service in the Spanish siege of Tortosa but the bulk reaching the Holy Land.

There they found the remnants of the great German and French land armies. Arriving close together at Constantinople in September and October 1147 after following the land route through central Europe, each was defeated by Turkish forces in Asia Minor. The large German force was destroyed near Dorylaeum in October, King Conrad narrowly escaping but wounded. The French, having earlier rejected an offer of sea transport by King Roger II of Sicily, although badly mauled in western Asia Minor in the winter of 1147–8, managed to reach the port of Adalia, only for Louis VII to abandon his infantry and sail directly to Syria with an army of officers but few men. The subsequent Holy Land campaign failed utterly. Conrad III managed to reconstruct some sort of army from the crusaders who had sailed from Lisbon. With Louis VII and the king of Jerusalem, Baldwin III (1143–63), he led an attack on Damascus (23–28 July 1148) that ended in a hasty enforced withdrawal as the Christians lacked the resources for a prolonged siege or to protect themselves from Muslim relief armies. The disaster led to bitter recriminations and accusations of treachery that scandalized the west, casting the whole idea of such expeditions in doubt.

## The Third Crusade, 1188–92

The four decades after the failed attack on Damascus in 1148 witnessed a gradual erosion of the strategic position of Outremer. The unification of Syria under Zengi's son, Nur al-Din of Aleppo (1146–74), the conquest of Egypt by his Kurdish mercenary commander Shirkuh (1168–9), and the creation of an Egypto-Syrian empire by Shirkuh's nephew, Saladin (1169–93), meant that by 1186 Outremer was surrounded. The rhetoric of this new, cohesive Muslim power placed great emphasis on *jihad* – war against infidels. This coincided with Outremer's financial weakness, lack of western aid and a descent, in the kingdom of Jerusalem, into debilitation and political instability. The royal succession passed in turn to a possible bigamist (Amalric 1163–74), a leper (Baldwin IV 1174–85), a child (Baldwin V 1185–6), and a woman (Sybil 1186–90) and her unpopular arriviste husband (Guy 1186–92). On 4 July 1187 Saladin annihilated the army of Jerusalem at the battle of Hattin in Galilee. Within a year almost all the Frankish ports and castles had surrendered or been captured; Jerusalem fell on 2 October 1187. Resistance was reduced largely to Tyre, Tripoli, and Antioch.

The response in the west was massive. By March 1188, the kings of Germany, France, and England had taken the cross with many of their leading nobles. King William II of Sicily had sent a fleet east. Preaching and recruitment had begun and campaign strategies carefully developed. A profits tax, known as the Saladin Tithe, had been instituted in France and the British Isles. In 1189, King Guy of Jerusalem, recently released from Saladin's captivity, began to besiege the vital port of Acre. For the next two years, this became the focal point of Christian military effort. In the same year fleets

8. The battle of Hattin, 4 July 1187. This fictional scene, drawn by the English monk Matthew Paris of St Alban's (d.1259), shows the moment when the relic of the True Cross the Franks bore into battle was seized by Saladin (crowned on the left) from the Christians led by King Guy (crowned in the centre, trying to cling onto the relic). This personalized depiction testifies to the impact of the event in memory as at the time.

from northern Europe began to arrive. In May 1189, Frederick Barbarossa, king of Germany and Holy Roman Emperor, set out at the head of an army allegedly 100,000 strong. After successfully forcing a passage through the unhelpful Byzantine Empire and the hostile Turkish Anatolia, Frederick's crusade ended in tragic bathos when he drowned trying to cross the River Saleph in Cilicia on 10 June 1190. Demoralized, his huge army disintegrated, only a small rump reaching Acre.

Although English and French contingents began sailing eastwards in 1189, the kings did not embark until 1190, delayed by political feuding over the succession to Henry II of England (d. July 1189). Given the delicate relationship caused by the English king holding extensive lands as a vassal of the French crown, King Philip II of France (1180–1223) and the new king of England, Richard I (1189–99), decided to travel together. Richard's skills as a general and administrator of men, ships, and materials and his vast reserves of cash soon elevated him to the central role in the crusade. Deflected not at all by anti-Jewish riots and massacres in English towns, notably York, in 1189–90, the kings departed in July 1190, making their rendezvous in September at Messina in Sicily, where they wintered. While Philip sailed for Acre in March 1191, arriving on 20 April, Richard's larger forces were blown off course to Cyprus. With elements in his army being mistreated by its independent Greek ruler, Richard took the opportunity to conquer the island in a lightning campaign in May. Cyprus remained in Christian hands until 1571. Richard finally arrived at Acre on 6 June 1191. After a further six weeks' hard pounding, the city surrendered on 12 July. On 31 July, Philip II abandoned the crusade, pleading illness and pressing business at home but clearly discomforted by Richard's dominance. Most of his followers showed what they thought of his action by staying. After executing hundreds of Muslim prisoners in his impatience at Saladin's prevarication over implementing the Acre surrender agreement, Richard began his march south towards Jerusalem on 22 August.

9. A portrait of Frederick I of Germany dressed as a crusader *c.*1188. The inscription urges him to fight the 'Saracens'. On the right the provost of Schäftlarn is presenting him with a copy of a popular history of the First Crusade by Robert of Rheims, a sign of how stories of past crusades influenced crusade mentalities and expectations.

The Palestine war of 1191–2 revolved around security. Since overwhelming victory eluded both sides, the only resolution lay in a sustainable political agreement. Richard I used force to try to frighten Saladin into restoring the pre-1187 kingdom of Jerusalem. If diplomacy succeeded, battles and sieges became unnecessary. The conflict was prolonged because neither side achieved sufficient military advantage to persuade the other to make acceptable concessions. On 7 September 1191, Richard repulsed Saladin's attempt to drive the crusaders into the sea at Arsuf, the major engagement of the campaign. Twice Richard marched his troops to within twelve miles of Jerusalem (January and June/July 1192) only to withdraw each time, arguing he had insufficient men to take or keep the city. These were prudent decisions but jarred with the reason why he was in southern Palestine in the first place. With Saladin failing to take the important port of Jaffa in late July 1192 and Richard unable to develop a scheme to attack Saladin's power base in Egypt, military stalemate dictated a diplomatic conclusion. Negotiations proved tortuous. Saladin refused to contemplate suggestions of any formal Christian authority within Jerusalem, but was otherwise prepared to accept a measure of Palestinian partition. The Treaty of Jaffa (2 September 1192) left the Franks in control of the coast from Acre to Jaffa and allowed access to Jerusalem for pilgrims and freedom of movement between Muslim and Christian territories. Ill and eager to return home, Richard sailed from Acre on 9 October. Ironically, Saladin died less than six months later (4 March 1193).

While failing to recapture Jerusalem, the Third Crusade determined the pattern for later eastern crusades. Thereafter, support for the reconstituted kingdom of Jerusalem, which lasted until 1291, came exclusively by sea. Cyprus provided a new and valuable partner for the Frankish settlements of the mainland. Diplomacy and truces between Muslims and Christians became standard practice. The subjugation of Egypt adopted centre stage in western strategic planning. Preaching and recruitment for crusading became increasingly professional, with finance being

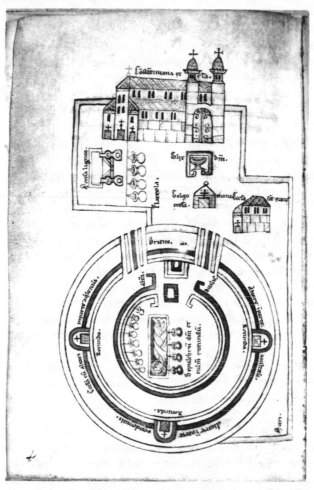

10. A 12th-century impressionistic ground plan of the Church of the Holy Sepulchre, with the shrine at the centre of the rotunda at the bottom. Such images penetrated widely in Christendom, inspiring journeys to Jerusalem and architectural imitations of the rotunda itself, a circular design seen in churches such as that of the Temple in London.

arranged by governments or the church through taxation. A more precise theology of violence refined the privileges and obligations of the crusaders themselves. After the failures of 1191–2, even the focus on Jerusalem shifted, the *iter Jerosolymitana* (Jerusalem journey) became subsumed into the *negotium terrae sanctae* (the business of the Holy Land), or simply the *sanctum negotium* (the holy business).

## The Fourth Crusade, 1198–1204

The thin strip of Palestinian coast restored to Christian rule by the Third Crusade proved a commercially viable base for a restored, if reduced, kingdom of Jerusalem over the following century, although the Holy City itself only returned to Christian rule between 1229 and 1244. After recovering much of the coast during the 1190s, the Franks found protection in a sequence of truces with Saladin's heirs in Egypt and Syria. Until the mid-13th century, western aid came largely on its own terms rather than in response to a specific crisis. The inception of the Fourth Crusade rested with Pope Innocent III (1198–1216), who envisaged all Christians as to some degree obliged to pursue the Lord's War. This Innocent promoted as part of the general devotional life of the west through preaching and the liturgy. An enthusiast for wars of the cross against a wide range of perceived threats to the church, Innocent regarded the recovery of the Holy Land as a central and urgent objective. One of the first things he did was to proclaim a new eastern expedition in August 1198.

By 1201, Innocent's call had been answered by a group of powerful northern French barons, including Count Baldwin of Flanders, who chose as their leader the well-connected northern Italian marquess Boniface of Montferrat, whose family had a long history of close involvement in the eastern Mediterranean. Egypt was chosen as the target of the expedition. The absence of kings denied the crusaders access to national taxes or fleets, forcing them to seek transport from Venice. Unfortunately, the agreement with Venice stipulated an optimistically large number of crusaders and a commensurately inflated price to be paid. It became apparent in the summer of 1202 that the crusaders, by now gathered at Venice, could not raise the agreed sum. As well as supplying 50 warships of their own, the Venetians had committed much of their shipping and hence annual income to carry the crusade. Realistically, they could neither abandon the enterprise nor cancel the debt. As a solution, the doge, Enrico Dandolo (d.1205), offered a moratorium on the debt in return for the crusaders' help in capturing the port of Zara in Dalmatia, even though this was a Christian city belonging to a fellow crusader, King Emeric of Hungary. Despite evident qualms and papal disapproval, the crusaders had little option if they wished to pursue their ultimate objective. Zara fell to the Veneto-crusader force on 24 November 1202.

By then, elements in the crusade and Venetian leadership were considering a further diversion to Constantinople in support of Alexius Angelus, son of the deposed Byzantine emperor Isaac II (1185–95). Young Alexius promised to subsidize the crusaders' attack on Egypt if they helped him take the Byzantine throne from his usurping uncle Alexius III (1195–1203). Many crusaders were disgusted by the plan and withdrew, but the leadership and the bulk of the army sailed with young Alexius and the Venetians to Constantinople, arriving in June 1203. A month later an amphibious assault on the city persuaded Alexius III to flee, allowing for the restoration of Isaac II with his son, now Alexius IV, as co-emperor. Their dependence on loutish westerners alienated Greek opinion, while their inability to honour Alexius' promise of subsidy and assistance undermined support from the crusaders. In January 1204 they were deposed, murdered, and replaced by Alexius V Ducas Murzuphlus, who began hostile manoeuvres against the crusaders. Faced with a crisis of survival, the western leaders decided to impose their will on the Greeks, in March 1204 agreeing to conquer and partition the Byzantine Empire. On 12–13 April, the crusaders breached the walls of the city. Alexius V fled and the victorious westerners were allowed three days of pillaging.

Although probably exaggerated, this atrocity has rung down the centuries in infamy. Within weeks a Latin emperor, Baldwin of Flanders, had been appointed and the territorial annexation of the Greek Empire begun. A year later, hopes of continuing the crusade to Egypt were abandoned. The Latin empire of Constantinople lasted until 1261; western occupation of parts of Greece for centuries. The precarious state of parts of the Frankish conquests in Greece prompted crusades to be proclaimed against the Greeks from 1231 until well into the 14th century.

The capture of Constantinople was not an accident; it had been considered by every major expedition since 1147. Successive popes had voiced disappointment at Greek failure to contribute to the recovery of the Holy Land. In the circumstances of 1202–3, conquest appeared viable; in the spring of 1204 necessary. However, it was never the ultimate object of the crusade, and for Venice marked a new departure into territorial instead of simply commercial imperialism. The diversion was a result of policy not conspiracy, its motives a mixture of pragmatism, idealism, and opportunism that characterized all other wars of the cross.

## The Fifth Crusade, 1213–29

More than its predecessors, the Fifth Crusade reflected the institutionalization of crusading in Christian society as envisaged by Innocent III. In the context of a wider process of semi-permanent evangelization, crusading acted as one manifestation of Christian revivalism. The papal bull *Quia Maior* (1213) launching the new eastern enterprise extended access to the crusade remission of sins, the indulgence, to those who sent a proxy or provided a proportionate sum of money in redemption of their vow. In 1215 the Fourth Lateran Council of the western Church authorized universal clerical taxation to support the cause. A massive and carefully orchestrated campaign of recruitment, propaganda, and finance produced a series of expeditions to the east between 1217 and 1229. The bulk of recruits came from Germany, central Europe, Italy, and the British Isles instead of France, the traditional heartland of crusade enlistment. After early contingents landed at Acre in 1217–18, including one led by King Andrew of Hungary (1205–35), the focus of military operations turned to Egypt when, in 1218, the crusaders attacked Damietta, a port in the eastern Nile Delta. The city fell only after a difficult and costly siege in November 1219. Egyptian proposals to exchange Damietta for Jerusalem were rejected as improper and unworkable by a group led by the Cardinal Legate, Pelagius, whose control of the purse strings gave him considerable authority within the crusade army. Lack of leadership proved more damaging. The westerners refused to accept orders from the king of Jerusalem, John of Brienne (1210–25). However, the commander chosen by the pope, Frederick II of Germany (1211–50), remained in Europe. In the summer of 1221, to prevent the crusade disintegrating through inactivity, the Christian army moved south towards Cairo, only to be cut off by floods, harried by the Egyptians, and forced to surrender on 30 August. Damietta was evacuated on 8 September 1221.

Recruiting continued almost unabated despite the setback in Egypt. In 1227, Frederick II finally embarked for the east, only to turn back immediately because of sudden and serious illness. Although Pope Gregory IX (1227–41), a veteran crusade recruiting agent, lost patience and excommunicated him, Frederick, undaunted, sailed to the Holy Land in 1228. Exploiting the rivalries between the rulers of Egypt and Syria, in February 1229 Frederick agreed a treaty with the sultan of Egypt that restored Jerusalem to the Franks. The city was to be open to all and the Haram al-Sharif, the Temple Mount, to remain under the Islamic religious authorities (not dissimilar to the arrangements in Jerusalem after 1967). However, unpopular for his high-handedness, when Frederick embarked for the west from Acre on 1 May 1229 he was pelted with offal. With a brief interruption in 1240, Jerusalem remained in Christian hands until captured by Khwarazmian raiders, Turkish freebooters in the pay of the sultan of Egypt, in 1244. The city remained under Muslim control until 1917.

# The 13th century

After 1229, eastern crusades progressed from the pragmatic to the optimistic to the desperate. Truces with feuding Muslim neighbours continued to sustain Frankish Outremer until the accession to power in Egypt of the militant Mamluk sultans, members of a professional caste of Turkish slave warriors, who replaced the heirs of Saladin in the 1250s. The Franks' alliance with the Mongols who invaded Syria in the late 1250s, followed by the Mongols' defeat by the Mamluks and withdrawal from the region in 1260, left them vulnerable to the new Egyptian sultan, Baibars (1260–77), who was committed to eradicating the Christian settlements. Successive western expeditions under a series of great nobles (the Count of Champagne in 1239; the Earl of Cornwall in 1240; the Lord Edward, later Edward I of England, in 1271) achieved little other than temporary advantage or respite. Rulers, such as the kings of France and Aragon, despatched occasional relief flotillas or stationed modest garrisons in Acre. Despite the continued popularity of crusading as an ideal and activity, between 1229 and the final loss of the last Christian outposts in Syria and Palestine in 1291, only one international campaign of substance reached the eastern Mediterranean, the crusade of Louis IX of France, 1248–54.

Louis IX's crusade proved the best prepared, most lavishly funded, and meticulously planned of all. It was also one of the most disastrous, its failure matching its ambition. Louis intended to conquer Egypt and change the balance of power in the Near East. Taking the cross in December 1244, over the next three years he assembled an army of about 15,000, a treasury of over 1 million *livres*, and a stockpile of food and equipment stored in Cyprus, where Louis arrived in the late summer of 1248. The following spring, supported by the Outremer Franks, Louis invaded Egypt, capturing Damietta the day he landed (5 June 1249). The assault on the interior began on 20 November, only to get bogged down in the Nile Delta for more than two months. After a hard-fought but indecisive engagement outside Mansourah on 7 February 1250,

Louis's army could make no further progress and became cut off from its base at Damietta. Withdrawal in early April turned into a rout as the Christian army disintegrated through disease, fatigue, and a superior enemy. Louis himself, suffering badly from dysentery, was among those captured, being released in return for Damietta and a massive ransom. Stunned by what he saw as God's chastisement, Louis remained in the Holy Land until 1254 bolstering defences (those at Caesarea can still be seen) and shoring up Outremer's diplomatic relations with its neighbours. Yet while securing his reputation for piety, Louis's stay did nothing to reverse the verdict of 1250. The best-laid crusade plan had failed dismally.

Following the defeat of the Mongols in 1260, Baibars of Egypt and his successors Qalawun (1279–90) and al-Ashraf Khalil (1290–3) systematically dismembered the remaining Frankish holdings in Syria and Palestine. Antioch fell in 1268; Tripoli in 1289; and, finally, after an heroic but futile defence, Acre in 1291, after which the remaining Christian outposts were evacuated without further resistance. To ensure the Franks would not again return, the sultans levelled the ports they captured. The west watched this collapse with alarm, concern, and impotence. Political rivalries, competing domestic demands, and a more realistic assessment of the required scale of operation conspired in the failure to organize adequate military response. Louis IX's new projected eastern expedition of 1270 reached no further than Tunis on its way to Egypt. There Louis died on 25 August 1270 and most of his followers went home. Yet after the final loss of Acre in 1291, plans continued to be hatched and raids conducted in the Levant throughout the 14th century until the new threat of the Ottoman Turks in the Balkans and the Aegean supervened from the 1350s and again in the mid-15th century, redirecting the focus of holy war.

# Chapter 3
# Crusades in the west

## Popular uprisings

The ideology and rhetoric of the Holy Land wars were applied easily to internal religious and political conflicts within Christendom and to frontier wars with non-Christians. Socially, its grip was exposed in the popular outbreaks of revivalist enthusiasm for the recovery of the Holy Land witnessed by the so-called Children's Crusade and the Shepherds' Crusades. The Children's Crusade in the summer of 1212 comprised two distinct outbursts of popular religious enthusiasm prompted by an atmosphere of crisis provoked by the preaching of the threats to Christendom simultaneously posed by the Muslims in the Holy Land, the Moors in Spain, and heretics in southern France. A series of penitential and revivalist processions in northern France, led by Stephen of Cloyes from the Vermandois, marched to St Denis near Paris voicing vague appeals for moral reform. There is no clear evidence these marchers intended to liberate Jerusalem. Further east, at much the same time, large groups of young men and adolescents (called in the sources *pueri*, meaning children but also anyone under full maturity) as well as priests and adults, apparently led by a boy called Nicholas of Cologne, marched through the Rhineland proclaiming their desire to free the Holy Sepulchre. It seems some of these marchers reached northern Italy seeking transport east but probably getting no further. Their holy war was of the spirit. Taking the church's teaching literally, they apparently believed their poverty, purity, and innocence would prevail where knights could not. Experience soon taught them otherwise.

The marches of 1212 found parallels in the Shepherds' Crusade of 1251, a populist rising in France that blamed Louis IX's Egyptian debacle on a corrupt nobility. Once its leaders were exposed not as holy men but disorderly rabble-rousers, the movement was violently suppressed. However, there were similar expressions of social and political anxieties through support for the transcendent cause of the Holy Land in Italy in 1309 and France in 1320. All were closely linked to news or rumours of external threats to Christendom, the dissemination of a clearly defined redemptive theology incorporating the crusade as a collective penitential act, and the perceived failure of the leaders of society to live up to their obligations on either count.

## Crusades against heretics and Christians

Official Church teaching increasingly encouraged the wide application of wars of the cross, even if Innocent III, in his bull *Quia Maior* (1213), was at pains to stress the priority of the Holy Land. From the 1130s Jerusalem indulgences on the model of 1096 were being offered to those fighting political enemies of the pope such as Roger II of Sicily (1101–54) or Markward of Anweiler in Sicily in 1199, assorted heretics, their protectors and mercenary bands. These indulgences were seemingly granted without the attendant vows, preaching, or cross-taking. The first time the full apparatus of the wars of the cross was directed against Christians came with the war declared by Innocent III in 1208 against the Cathar heretics of Languedoc, known later as the Albigensians, and their Christian protectors. One of the most notorious of all medieval wars, the Albigensian Crusades (1209–29) degenerated from a genuine attempt to cauterize widespread heresy, which many saw as a dangerously infectious wound bleeding all Christendom, into a brutal land seizure. The puritanical dualist Cathar heresy had grown in strength in parts of Languedoc controlled by the count of Toulouse. The assassination of the Papal Legate for the region in 1208 led Innocent III to offer Holy Land indulgences and the cross to northern French barons. Under a militant monkish zealot, Arnald-Amaury, abbot of Cîteaux, and an ambitious adventurer, Simon de Montfort, the crusaders began to annex the county of Toulouse and its surrounding provinces, often with great savagery meted out indiscriminately to local Christians as well as heretics. The sack of Béziers in 1209 was remembered as especially brutal. In 1213, Simon defeated and killed the count of Toulouse's ally King Peter of Aragon at the battle of Muret. After Simon's death in 1218, the impetus of the crusade faltered until revived by King Louis VIII of France (1223–6) in 1226. By the end of the year Languedoc had effectively been conquered, its subjugation confirmed in the Treaty of Paris (1229).

Ironically, for all its ultimate political success, the Albigensian Crusade failed to eradicate the Cathars, a task effected by the more pacific and reasoned methods of the Inquisition. However, crusades against heretics remained in the Church's arsenal for the rest of the Middle Ages and beyond. Six crusades were launched or planned against the Czech Hussite evangelicals of Bohemia between 1420 and 1471. Protestant Reformations in the 16th century stimulated a revival of crusade schemes against enemies of the Catholic Church, such as Henry VIII and Elizabeth I of England, and remained a traditional resort for devout and threatened Catholics in the new Wars of Religion, for example against the Huguenots in France in the 1560s.

To assert and sustain the 13th-century papacy's plenitude of power, drive for doctrinal and liturgical uniformity, and acquisition of a temporal state in Italy, popes found the crusade a malleable instrument. Those attacked by *crucesignati* as 'schismatics' included peasants in the Netherlands and the Lower Weser (1228–34); Bosnians opposed to Hungarian rule (from 1227); and rebels against the pope's vassal Henry III of England (1216–17 and

1265). The main crusades against Christians were fought over papal security in its lands in Italy. From the 1190s, popes were fearful of being surrounded by the Hohenstaufen dynasty, kings of Germany who were also rulers of southern Italy and Sicily. This caused the Thirty Years' War with the Hohenstaufen Frederick II and his heirs (1239–68) that ended with a papal nominee, Charles of Anjou, as ruler of Sicily and Naples. Following a Sicilian rebellion against Charles in 1282, much of the fighting during the Wars of the Sicilian Vespers (1282–1302) also attracted the apparatus of crusading: cross, preaching, indulgences, church taxation, and so on. This habit continued for the regular local or regional campaigns in pursuit of papal interests in central and northern Italy during the popes' residence at Avignon (1309–77). These Italian crusades scarcely pretended to conceal papal corporate or personal interest, to the disgust of critics such as Dante. The failure of crusades launched by both contending parties to end the Great Papal Schism (1378–1417) led to the abandonment of this form of holy war, only occasionally to be revived by bellicose popes such as Julius II (1503–13).

## Spain

The ceremonies and privileges associated with expeditions to Jerusalem had been extended to cover those fighting the Muslims in Spain since the 1090s, a process regularized by the First Lateran Council in 1123. Further authorization for crusades against the Moors came in 1147–8, during the Second Crusade, and at intervals thereafter. A church council in Segovia in 1166 even offered Jerusalem indulgences to those who defended Castile from Christian attack. The later 12th-century invasions of Iberia by the Muslim fundamentalist Almohads from North Africa threatened Christian conquests and provoked a greater frequency in crusading appeals, culminating in the crusade of 1212 against them. This led to the great Christian victory of Las Navas de Tolosa (1212) over the Almohads. Thereafter the campaigns of the Spanish Reconquista became more obviously national concerns, although still liable to

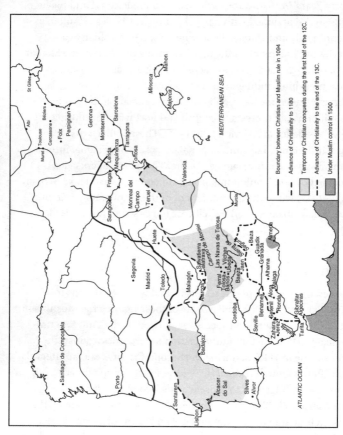

E. The Spanish Reconquista

Boundary between Christian and Muslim rule in 1094

Advance of Christianity to 1180

Temporary Christian conquests during the first half of the 12C.

Advance of Christianity to the end of the 13C.

Under Muslim control in 1500

MEDITERRANEAN SEA

ATLANTIC OCEAN

St Gilles
Albi
Toulouse
Muret
Carcassonne
Foix
Perpignan
Gerona
Barcelona
Montserrat
Tarragona
Lérida
Mequinenza
Tortosa
Fraga
Monreal del Campo
Saragossa
Valencia
Teruel
Huete
Segovia
Madrid
Toledo
Malagón
Alarcos
Calatrava de Montiel
Campo
Las Navas de Tolosa
Tolosa
Ferral
Vilches
Baños Úbeda
Baeza
Jaén
Córdoba
Baza
Guadix
Granada
Almería
Alhama
Málaga
Seville
Benamejí
Setenil
Aloya
Ronda
Zahara
Jerez
Gibraltar
Algeciras
Tarifa
Santiago de Compostela
Porto
Badajoz
Santarém
Alcácer do Sal
Silves
Alvor
Lisbon
Santarém
Minorca
Mahon
Majorca
Murcia

elicit crusade status, as with the conquests of the Balearic Islands (1229–31) and Valencia (1232–5) by James I of Aragon (1213–76).

With the fall of Cordova (1236) and Seville (1248) to Ferdinand III of Castile (1217–52), formal or active crusading against the Moors, now penned in the emirate of Granada (until 1492), became effectively redundant. Ironically, the peninsula's most intimate subsequent experience of crusading was as victim when the French invaded Aragon in 1285 as part of the crusade called at the start of the War of Sicilian Vespers (1282–1302).

## The Baltic

The Baltic crusades acted as one element in a cruel process of Christianization and Germanization, providing a religious gloss to ethnic cleansing and territorial aggrandizement more blatant and, in places, more successful than anywhere else. Crusading in the Baltic, first applied to Danish and German anti-Slav aggression between the Elbe and Oder in 1147 during the Second Crusade, cloaked a missionary war which, given the Christian prohibition on forced conversion, represented a contradiction in canon law. These wars directly served local political and ecclesiastical ambitions. The main areas of conquest after 1200 included Prussia, Livonia, Estonia, and Finland. In Prussia, the expansion of land-grabbing German princes in Pomerania gave way to the competing interests of Denmark and the Military Order of Teutonic Knights. This order had originally been founded by Germans in Acre in the wake of the Third Crusade in the 1190s, but because of its regional associations soon became heavily, and ultimately almost exclusively, involved in fighting for the cross in the north. The fighting in Livonia devolved onto the church under the archbishop of Riga and the Military Order of Sword Brothers (founded in 1202). In Estonia the Danes again clashed with the Military Orders, as well as with Swedes and Russians from Novgorod. Finland became the target of Swedish expansion. By the 1230s, control of war and settlement in Prussia, Livonia, and southern Estonia had been taken up by the Teutonic

11. Moors fighting Christians in 13th-century Spain. The artist is at pains to show a (probably exaggerated) contrast in weapons, shields, and armour between the two sides.

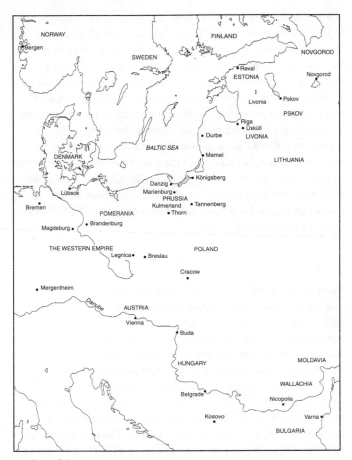

**F. The Baltic**

Knights, with whom the Sword Brothers were amalgamated in 1237. In 1226 their Master, Hermann von Salza, was created imperial prince of Prussia, which was declared a papal fief held by the Teutonic Knights in 1234. Although some specific grants for crusades in the Baltic continued, most of these northern wars adopted the character of 'eternal crusades' once Innocent IV in 1245

49

confirmed the right of the Teutonic Knights to grant crusade indulgences without special papal authorization. This gave the Teutonic Knights a unique status, not held even by the rulers of the kingdom of Jerusalem, of a sovereign government possessed of the automatic right of equating its foreign policy with the crusade. Cashing in on this in the 14th century, the Knights developed a sort of chivalric package tour for western nobles eager to see some fighting, enjoy lavish feasting, earn indulgences, and gild their reputations. The Knights' appeal slackened with their failure to overcome Lithuania-Poland and the conversion of pagan Lithuania in 1386. Their transformation into a secular German principality was completed in 1525 when the Master of the Teutonic Knights in Prussia embraced Lutheranism and secularization. The Livonian branch followed suit in 1562.

## Jews

Frontiers, medieval or modern, can be religious, ethnic, cultural, and social as well as geographic. In such cases, wars of the cross added a particular edge of hostility or intensity. While no crusades were specifically directed against the Jewish communities anywhere in Europe or Asia, the ideology of crusading encouraged violence against them, despite official secular and ecclesiastical disapproval. The ringing condemnation of enemies of the cross and the concentration on the Crucifixion story in the preaching of Urban II in 1095–6, or Bernard of Clairvaux's in 1146–7, needed little misunderstanding to be applied to the Jews. The pogroms in the Rhineland in 1096 and 1146–7 and in England in 1190 were not the sum of anti-Jewish violence, which spread widely in northern Europe. But the Jews were only ever collateral targets of crusading. Local rulers reserved exploitation and expropriation to themselves; Richard I condemned the attacks on Jews in London in 1189 because he regarded their property as his. A cultural myopia on the part of Christians refused to see Jews as fully human, a dismissive attitude prominently displayed by the great crusader Louis IX of France. Such discrimination could translate into persecution, although increasingly it led to expulsion from regions of the British Isles and France in the later 13th and 14th centuries. Lacking civil rights or in most cases effective systems of autonomous rule or defence, Jews in medieval Europe suffered through Christian schizophrenia. Protected by Christian Biblical prescript, Jews were politically not sufficiently visible to constitute the sort of material threat that would elicit a crusade against them. Yet at the same time Christian teaching also saw them as malign and therefore a religious challenge to Christianity. Increasingly, blood libels, accusations of Jews murdering Christians, rather than crusades, provoked massacres. Where daily experience and long tradition denied both Jewish malignity and cultural invisibility, as, ironically, in two regions most infected by active crusading, Spain and Outremer, Jews were less molested, even tolerated. Crusading played a part, at times a gory one, in constructing a closed, intolerant society. However, to blame the excesses of anti-Semitism, medieval or modern, on the wars of the cross is facile and unconvincing. That well of hatred fed from many streams.

## The end of crusading

The traditional terminal date for the Crusades, the loss of Acre in 1291, makes no sense. People continued to take the cross, if in diminishing numbers. The attendant institutions of indulgences, legal obligations, and taxation persisted in use by rulers and popes for centuries. At least until the outbreak of the Hundred Years' War in the 1330s, the recovery of the Holy Land seemed viable, if difficult and expensive. In the Mediterranean, attacks on piratical Turkish emirs and the Mamluks continued sporadically, such as the sack of Alexandria in 1365 by Peter I of Cyprus. The growing power of the Ottoman Turks from the mid-14th century redefined the objective of crusading, throwing Christendom once more on the defensive. At Nicopolis on the Danube (1396) and Varna on the Black Sea (1444) western crusade armies sent to combat the Ottomans in the Balkans were crushed, on both occasions with the Turks receiving aid from Christian allies, respectively Serbs and

Genoese. Rhodes, occupied by the Military Order of St John, the Hospitallers, since 1309, held out until 1522 before relocating to Malta, from where they were evicted by Napoleon in 1798. Cyprus remained in Christian hands until 1571, Crete until 1669; both fruits of earlier crusades. Crusading mentalities were re-forged in the Adriatic and central Europe in the face of the Ottoman advance in the 15th century. After the Turkish capture of Constantinople in 1453, crusading again seemed a vital necessity to the Renaissance papacy. In response to the fall of the Greek imperial capital a new crusade was proclaimed. Belgrade was saved in 1456 by an unlikely crusading force gathered by John of Capistrano. As long as the Ottomans presented a danger, crusading ideas retained relevance and interest, even into the 17th century, when Francis Bacon dismissed them as 'the rendezvous of cracked brains that wore their feather in their head instead of their hat'. Yet the appeal lingered. Men may have taken the cross and expected indulgences in the anti-Turkish Holy League (1684–97). The end of crusading came not in the drama of a failed campaign or a siege lost, but as a long, dying fall, finally obliterated as kingdoms and secular powers, not churches or religion, claimed the morality as well as control of warfare.

# Chapter 4
# The impact of the Crusades

Traditionally, the crusades outside Christendom have been credited with profound influence over the distribution of political and religious power in the regions they affected. Yet their impact as well as success was determined by forces usually beyond the crusaders' control. Without the disintegration of the unity of the Muslim Near East in the late 11th century and of Muslim Spain two generations earlier, wars of the cross against Islam would probably not have begun or would have rapidly stalled. Conversely, without the westerners' political and economic capacity to sustain conquest and colonization, in the Mediterranean and the Baltic, these wars would have proved evanescent. The 13th-century failure of the Muslim powers of North Africa and southern Iberia and of the disparate tribes of the southern and eastern Baltic to maintain any concerted resistance to Christian expansion allowed crusades to prevail. In marked contrast stood the rise of Lithuania in the 14th century that successfully resisted further crusading advances in the Baltic, a unification comparable strategically to that of Syria, Palestine, and Egypt under the Ayyubids (c.1174–1250) and the Mamluks (1250–1517) which sealed the fate of Outremer.

The consequences of crusading activity varied hugely. In Spain, the Christian reconquest decisively reoriented the political and cultural direction of the region. In the Baltic, the conquest and Christianization of Prussia, Livonia, and Finland redefined the area and its peoples within Latin Christendom. In Greece and its islands,

12. A medieval world map, from a 14th-century copy of the Englishman Ranulph Higden's encyclopaedic *Polychronicon*. Typically, Jerusalem is shown at the centre, the navel of the world. (East is at the bottom.)

large areas of which were occupied by western nobles and Venetians after the Fourth Crusade, in some cases for centuries, the effect of western conquest tended to be superficial, but while it lasted, as in the case of Venetian Crete (held until 1669), often unpleasant or

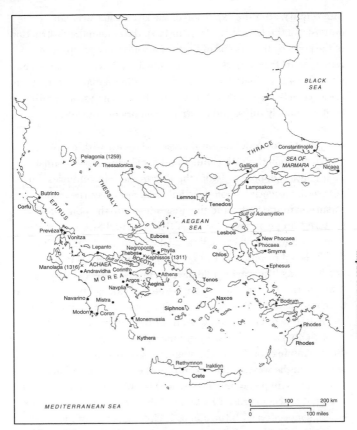

**G. The Aegean in the 13th and 14th centuries**

downright brutal for the indigenous population. By contrast, in the Near East, with the exception of Cyprus which fell to Richard I of England in 1191 and remained in the hands of Latin Christians until 1571, the western presence that had begun when the first crusaders burst into Anatolia and northern Syria in the summer and autumn of 1097 left few traces except physical and, possibly, cultural scars. Although western-sponsored coastal raids continued into the

15th century, after the expulsion of the last Latin Christian outposts on the Levantine shore in 1291, the systematic destruction of the ports by the sultans of Egypt prevented any prospect of return, apart from a trickle of determined, well-heeled pilgrims and a few friars as resident tourist guides. Nothing remains of the Latin presence in Syria and Palestine except stones, some still standing as built but mostly ruins, and a revived memory of bitterness.

It is possible to argue that suppression of heresy within Christendom in the 13th century and papal campaigns against their political opponents from the 13th to the 15th centuries did not require a special ideology of holy war. Similarly, the frontier expansion in the Baltic and the integration into the polity of western Europe of powers such as Denmark and Sweden preceded their association with crusading ideology and practices. In Spain, the Christian reconquest, or Reconquista, predated its reinvention as a holy war. The wars would have occurred in any case. By contrast, the wars in the eastern Mediterranean can be seen only as the consequence of this new form of holy war. Geographically, Syria and Palestine did not lie on western Christendom's frontiers. Only through imaginative empathy did the politics of the Near East directly impinge on Latin Christendom, a consequence of the ubiquity in the west's religious culture of endless repetition of the Bible stories, in preaching, liturgy, and the plastic arts. Perhaps the strangest aspect of crusading to the Holy Land lay precisely in its lack of connection with the domestic circumstances of the territories whither the armies were directed. While the First Crusade answered the interests of the eastern Greek Christian empire of Byzantium, it was hardly portrayed as such and developed a momentum quite removed from Greek frontier policy. There existed no strategic or material interest for the knights of the west to campaign in Judaea. This is where comparisons with modern imperialism collapse. For the land-hungry or politically ambitious adventurer, other regions nearer home offered easier, richer pickings. With the partial exception of the Third Crusade (1188–92), currents of western enthusiasm and policy, as in the

Fourth and Fifth Crusades, determined the timing and recruitment of eastern crusades rather than the immediate needs of the western settlements in the Levant. More generally, while the presence of western warriors and settlers on the immediate frontiers of Muslim Iberia or the pagan Baltic made some economic or political sense, this was not true for the Holy Land, where the motive for occupation depended on its status as a relic of Christ on earth, a fundamentally religious mission however material the methods employed to achieve it. Consequently, the Christian wars of the 12th and 13th centuries in the Near East provide startling testimony to the power of ideas.

## The Crusades and Muslim power

How significant, therefore, were these eastern crusades in the development of international patterns of power? They certainly thrust westerners into geopolitical events otherwise far removed from their orbit of interest. A particular religious perception of world history led to western European involvement in fashioning the political destiny of Syria, Palestine, Egypt, and Iraq in a period of decisive re-alignment of Near Eastern power.

Urban II possessed an acute interest in Christian political history, which often made gloomy reading. The successes of the acceptance of Christianity by the Roman Empire in the 4th century and the subsequent conversion of the Germanic successor powers in the ruins of the western empire from the 5th to 7th centuries had been offset by the irruption of Islam in the 7th and early 8th centuries. The rapid Arab conquests of the Christian provinces of Egypt, Palestine and Syria, North Africa, and most of the Iberian peninsula between 634 and 711 had reduced Christendom, as one late medieval pope had it, to an 'angle of the world'. Jerusalem had fallen to Arab rule in 638; almost all the Biblical scenes familiar to the faithful lay under Muslim control. Further advances in the 9th century, including the capture of Sicily and bases in southern Italy, seemed to threaten Rome and convert the western Mediterranean into a Muslim lake. The two most powerful regimes in the west, the Carolingian Empire of the 8th century or the German emperors of the 10th and 11th, despite laying claims to an Italian kingdom, rarely engaged directly with the loss of southern Christian provinces. For the empire of Byzantium, with its long frontiers with Islamic states, the confrontation occupied a habitual rather than urgent element of foreign policy, especially after the stabilization of borders in eastern Anatolia from the 8th century.

The hundred years before 1095 saw a transformation. In the western Mediterranean, Muslim pirates were ejected from bases in southern France at the end of the 10th century. Between 1061 and 1091, Italian-Norman forces conquered Sicily. Further west, the collapse of the caliphate of Cordova in Spain in 1031 and its replacement by a patchwork of competing principalities, ruled by the so-called *taifa* (or 'party') kings, presented Christian rulers and mercenaries from outside the peninsula with opportunities to extract tribute and extend territory. Driven by politics and profit, not religion, Christian rule advanced piecemeal, Muslim–Christian alliances being as common as conflict. The famed conqueror of Valencia in 1094, the Castilian Roderigo Diaz (d.1099), 'El Cid', spent as much of his career fighting for Muslim lords against Christians as vice versa. However, when the usually squabbling Christian princes united, significant gains were achieved, notably the capture of Toledo by Alfonso VI of Castile in 1085. Dynastic and ecclesiastical links drew recruits from Catalonia and north of the Pyrenees, although only with hindsight could they be equated with crusaders.

In the eastern Mediterranean in the second half of the 10th century, Byzantine armies had re-established a foothold in northern Syria, capturing Antioch in 969, which remained in Greek hands until 1084, only a decade and a half before the arrival of the First Crusade. Otherwise, the Anatolian/Syrian frontiers had remained largely static. The tripartite balance of power in the region was based on the Byzantine Empire to the north and west; the orthodox Sunni Muslim Abbasid Caliphate of Baghdad in nominal control of

Iran, Iraq, and Syria; with the Shia Muslim Caliphate of the
Fatimids in Egypt since 969. In the 11th century the political
configuration of the Near East was severely jolted by the eruption of
the Seljuk Turks from northeast Iran. Establishing themselves in
control of the Baghdad Caliphate in 1055 as sultans (*sultan* is
Arabic for power), the Seljuks pushed further west, by 1079
establishing their overlordship in most of Syria and Palestine,
having in 1071 defeated a Byzantine army at Manzikert in
northeastern Anatolia. Within twenty years, a Seljuk Sultanate had
been consolidated in Anatolia with a capital at Nicaea close to
Constantinople. However, despite the Seljuk conquests, Muslim
unity was a charade, especially after the outbreak of civil war
between the heirs of Sultan Malik Shah. The Seljuk empire in Iraq
and Syria comprised a loose confederation of city states, often
controlled by Turkish military commanders (*atabegs*) and slave
mercenaries (*Mamluks*) who owed allegiance to one or other rival
Seljuk prince. Throughout the region ethnic diversity and
alienation of ruler from ruled prevailed. In parts of Syria,
immigrant Turkish Sunnis ruled an indigenous Shia population or
forced their protection on local Arab dynasts. The Shia Fatimid
Caliphate of Egypt, with power in the hands of often non-Arab,
Turkish or Armenian viziers, ruled a largely Sunni population. Such
complexity ensured a continuing political volatility that offered rich
opportunities to the ambitious, the ruthless, the skilful, and the
fortunate. The appearance of the western armies of the First
Crusade in 1097–8 merely added one more foreign military
presence to an area already crowded with competing rulers from
outside the region.

In contrast with the impact of wars of the cross in and around
western Europe, the conquests in Syria and Palestine played only a
modest role in defining the political direction of the Near East in
the 12th and 13th centuries and none thereafter. Developments
beyond the Muslim frontiers and Christian control largely
determined the settlers' fate. The 12th century witnessed the
establishment first of Syrian unity under Zengi of Aleppo (d.1146)

13. Mamluk warriors training. The Mamluks were professional Turkish mercenaries enlisted as warrior slaves in the armies of Egypt who took control of the country after 1250 and drove the Franks from the mainland of Syria and Palestine in 1291.

and his son Nur al-Din (d.1174) and then of the unification of Syria with Egypt under Nur al-Din's Kurdish mercenary commander turned independent Egyptian sultan, Saladin (d.1193). Apart from a serious attempt to contest control of Egypt between 1163 and 1169, the Christian rulers in Palestine, the Franks, observed the process as largely impotent bystanders. Only after he had secured the three inland Muslim capitals of Damascus, Aleppo, and Mosul did Saladin turn his armies on the Franks in the crushing campaign of 1187–8 that gave rise to the Third Crusade.

Although Saladin, Zengi, and Nur al-Din all located their policies in the vanguard of a Muslim religious revival that swept westwards from Iran and Iraq, decking their wars with the language of *jihad*, most of their energies and violence was directed both materially and ideologically against other Muslims. Saladin's capture of Jerusalem in 1187 was matched by his suppression of the heretical Fatimid Caliphate in 1171. For Saladin and his successors, their main concerns focused on the internal maintenance of their empire, reflected in Saladin's pragmatic approach to negotiating the partition of Palestine with the Franks during the Third Crusade. The repeated civil wars among Saladin's successors, the Ayyubids, encouraged them to enter into truces with the Franks, who still controlled much of the Syro-Palestinian coast between the 1190s and 1260s. Beyond temporary panics following their capture of Damietta (1219 and 1249), the Ayyubid military system successfully resisted the two Christian attacks on Egypt (1218–21 and 1249–50), although in 1250 the role in defending Egypt played by corps of Mamluk mercenaries precipitated their assumption of the Egyptian sultanate. The advent of the Mamluks, by origin Turks from the Eurasian steppes, conformed to the pattern of alien rule in the Near East, as did the chief challenge to their new empire, the Mongols, who by the late 1250s had penetrated Iraq and Syria. Baghdad had been sacked and the last caliph executed in 1258; Frankish Antioch had become a client and Syria briefly occupied. The defeat of a Mongol army by the Mamluks of Egypt in September 1260 at Ain Jalut in the valley of Jezreel helped determine which of the two dominant Near Eastern forces would rule in Syria and roughly where the frontier between them would fall in a political settlement that lasted until the Ottoman conquest of the Mamluk Empire in 1517. The Franks and their western allies could only watch.

The final expulsion of the Franks, begun by the fearsome Baibars and completed by al-Ashraf Khalil in 1291, carried a negative charge generated by the conquerors not the Franks themselves. In annexing the Christian strongholds of the coast, the Mamluks deliberately razed them to the ground, thereby, in H. E. Mayer's words, achieving the 'destruction of the ancient Syro-Palestinian city civilisation'. The decisive verdicts of 1260 and 1291 crowned the Mamluks as victors in the long struggle over which foreign group would rule in Egypt, Syria, and Palestine – Greeks, Kurds, Turks, Franks. The last were merely one of many who lost out; their role in the reconfiguration of the political map intrusive, not decisive.

Steven Runciman, the most read anglophone historian of the Crusades, thought the Crusades proved to be a disaster for Christendom because the Byzantine Empire was weakened as a result of the Fourth Crusade. Permanently undermined, Byzantium 'could no longer guard Christendom against the Turk', this incapacity ultimately handing 'the innocent Christians of the Balkans' to 'persecution and slavery'. Yet it may be worth considering that the victory of the Mamluks in the second half of the 13th century saved not only western Asia from the Mongols but southern and eastern Europe too. The failure of Byzantium to defend itself in 1203–4 did not augur well for any putative role as a bastion against future Turkish attacks; the occupation of parts of the Greek Empire by Franks and Venetians at least ensured lasting western investment in the later resistance to the Ottomans. Its disastrous failure to accommodate the crusaders before 1204 makes it hard to believe Byzantium left to itself would have coped any better with the Turks. While scarcely interested in the minutiae of local politics and religion, the Mongols might have proved even more disagreeable conquerors than the Ottomans.

Although fatal to the Franks of Outremer, the Mamluk triumph restricted the Mongols to Persia and preserved an Islamic status quo that can only be condemned on grounds of race or religion. Precisely the same can be said of those who assume the malignity of Ottoman rule or that fractious Christian rule in the Balkans would have proved more beneficial to their inhabitants. While easy to re-fight the Crusades in modern historical or cultural prejudices, it remains unprofitable if not actually harmful. One legacy of the Crusades was the estrangement of Greek and Latin Christendom, but not the triumph of the Turk.

# Chapter 5
# Holy war

Christian holy war, although a conceptual oxymoron, has
occupied a central place in the culture of Christianity. Crusading
represented merely one expression of this warrior tradition.
Urban II did not invent Christian holy wars in 1095; neither
did they cease with the demise of the Crusades; nor were the
Crusades the only manifestation of medieval religious violence.
However, the Crusades have appeared almost uniquely disreputable
because of the apparent diametric and exultant reversal of the
teaching of Christ and the appropriation of the language of
spiritual struggle and the doctrine of peace for the promotion
of war, exquisitely demonstrated in the ubiquitous use of the
image of the cross. In the New Testament seemingly the ultimate
symbol of Christ's explicit refusal to fight or even resist in the
face of death; in the hands of crusade propagandists the cross
became a sign of obedience through the physical sacrifice of
martial combat, a war banner, an icon of military victory
through faith, the mark of those, in the words of a charter of
one departing crusader in 1096, who fought 'for God against
pagans and Saracens' and saw themselves as 'milites Christi',
warriors or knights of Christ. 'If any man will come after me,
let him deny himself and take up his cross, and follow me'
(Matthew 16:24) appears an incredible battle-cry in the context
of Christ's words in Gethsemane (Matthew 26:52–4): 'Put up
again thy sword . . . all they that take the sword shall perish with
the sword.'

This transformation can be illustrated startlingly in the writings of Bernard of Clairvaux (d.1153), chief propagandist and recruiting agent for the Second Crusade, one of the most influential interpreters of Christian spirituality of the entire Middle Ages. As if to counter directly those who condemned the church's advocacy of holy war as unchristian, Bernard took New Testament passages and radically reinterpreted them. The Epistles of St Paul used military metaphor to emphasize the revolutionary nature of the new faith in contrast to the Roman world dominated by religiously sanctioned military systems: 'We do not war after the flesh: for the weapons of our warfare are not carnal' (II Corinthians: 3–4). In the Epistle to the Ephesians Paul descants on this spiritual military theme:

> Put on the whole armour of God, that ye may be able to stand against the wiles of the devil. For we wrestle not against flesh and blood . . . Stand therefore, having your loins girt about with truth, and having on the breastplate of righteousness, and your feet shod with the preparation of the gospel of peace . . . taking the shield of faith . . . and take the helmet of salvation, and the sword of the spirit, which is the word of God.
>
> (Ephesians 6:11–17)

Bernard redirects Paul in his tract welcoming the founding of the Templars, 'a new sort of knighthood . . . fighting indefatigably a double fight against flesh and blood as well as against the immaterial forces of evil in the skies'; 'the knight who puts the breastplate of faith on his soul in the same way as he puts a breastplate of iron on his body is truly intrepid and safe from everything . . . so forward in safety, knights, and with undaunted souls drive off the enemies of the Cross of Christ'. While not entirely new – similar transmutations of Paul's spiritual armour date back to the 8th century at least – the volte face seems complete.

# Scripture and Classical theory

The ideology of crusading may thus appear casuistic in its interpretation of Scripture, if not downright mendacious. Yet the contradiction of holy war in pursuit of the doctrines of peace and forgiveness boasted long pedigrees. While remaining a utopian model, the behaviour and circumstances of the Early Church soon ceased to reflect the idealism or experiences of Christianity. Although Biblical authority remained one of the cornerstones of belief, literalism proved intellectually and culturally untenable and Christianity evolved only indirectly as a Scriptural faith. The foundation texts of the Old and New Testaments needed translation, literally and conceptually, to nurture accessible and sustainable institutions of thought and observance in a context of the lives of active believers within a temporal church. The works of the so-called Church Fathers (notably Origen of Alexandria, Ambrose of Milan, Augustine of Hippo, and Pope Gregory I) found ways of reconciling the purist doctrine of the Beatitudes with the Graeco-Roman world. A mass of apocryphal scripture, imitative hagiography, legends, relic cults, and lengthening tradition expressed, informed, and developed popular belief, while ecclesiastical and political authorities codified articles of faith, such as the Nicene Creed (325). The church's teaching on war exemplified this process.

The charity texts of the New Testament insisting on forgiveness were interpreted as applicable only to private persons not the behaviour of public authorities, to whom, both Gospel and Pauline texts could be marshalled to show, obedience was due. In Jerome's Latin version of the Bible, the Vulgate (c.405), which became the standard text in the medieval west, the exclusive word for enemy in the New Testament is *inimicus*, a personal enemy, not *hostis*, a public enemy. Paul, conceding that 'kings and those in authority' protect the faithful in 'a quiet and peaceable life', sanctioned public violence to police a sinful world. For those justifying religious war, the Old Testament supplied rich pickings. In contrast to modern

Christians not of Biblical fundamentalist persuasion, the medieval church placed considerable importance on the Old Testament for its apparent historicity, its moral stories, its prophecies, and its prefiguring of the New Covenant, as in the 13th-century stained glass windows in the nave of Chartres Cathedral where Old Testament scenes are coupled by their exegetical equivalents from the New. Bible stories operated essentially on two levels (although medieval exegetes distinguished as many as four): literal and divine truth. In the Old Testament the Chosen People of the Israelites fight battles for their faith and their God, who commands violence, protects his loyal warriors, and is Himself 'a man of war' (Exodus 15:3). Not only does God intervene directly, but He instructs His agents to kill: Moses enlisting the Levites to slaughter the followers of the Golden Calf (Exodus 32:26–8); God instructing Saul to annihilate the Amalekites 'men and women, infant and suckling' (I Samuel 15:3). Warrior heroes adorn the Scriptural landscape – Joshua, Gideon, David. In the Books of the Maccabees, recording the battles of Jews against the rule of Hellenic Seleucids and their Jewish allies in the 2nd century BC, butchery and mutilation are praised as the work of God through His followers, whose weapons are blessed and who meet their enemies with hymns and prayers. 'So, fighting with their hands and praying to God in their hearts, they laid low no less than thirty-five thousand and were greatly gladdened by God's manifestation' (II Maccabees 15:27–8). Many Old Testament texts, especially those concerning Jerusalem (for example Psalm 79: 'O God, the heathen are come into thine inheritance; thy holy temple have they defiled; they have laid Jerusalem on heaps', were easily incorporated into crusading apologetics and polemic, but nowhere was the idiom of crusading more apparent than in the Books of the Maccabees.

Of course, stories regarded by some as authorizing legitimate or even religious warfare could be interpreted by others as prefiguring Christian spiritual struggle, the sense of St Paul as well as many medieval commentators, or consigned to the Old Covenant not the New Dispensation. Trickier for Christian pacifists were the apocalyptic passages in the New Testament. The Revelation of St John described a violent Last Judgement when celestial armies followed 'The Word of God' and judged, made war, smote nations, and trod 'the winepress of the fierceness and wrath of Almighty God' (Revelation 19:11–15). It is no coincidence that one of the most famous and vivid eyewitness descriptions of the massacre in Jerusalem on 15 July 1099 quoted verbatim Revelation 14:20: 'And the winepress was trodden without the city, and blood came out of the winepress, even unto the horses' bridles.' Apart from examples of godly mayhem, the Bible imposed a generally providential and specifically prophetic dimension on Christian holy war that is hard to underestimate. If wars are seen as God's will, then they act as part of His scheme, either in imitation of past religious wars or, more potently, as fulfilment of Biblical prophecy, a fixation as appealing to crusaders as later to Oliver Cromwell.

Christian holy war, therefore, derived from the Bible its essential elements: Divine command; identification with the Israelites, God's chosen; and a sense of acting in events leading towards the Apocalypse. The historical and emotional vision of the holy warrior encompassed the temporal and supernatural. The fighting was only too material but the purpose was transcendent. However, it is difficult to see how even the most bellicose interpretation of Scripture alone could have produced such an acceptance and later promotion of warfare without the need to reconcile Christianity with the Roman state in the 4th and 5h centuries AD. While the Bible bore witness to the Law of God, old and new, the Helleno-Roman tradition had developed laws of man on which Christian writers drew to devise a new theoretical justification for war. Aristotle, in the 4th century BC, had coined the phrase 'just war' to describe war conducted by the state 'for the sake of peace' (Politics I:8 and VII:14). To this idea of a just end, Roman law added the just cause consequent on one party breaking an agreement (*pax*, peace, derived from the Latin *pangere*, meaning to enter into a contract) or injuring the other. Just war could therefore be waged for defence, recovery of rightful property, or punishment provided this was sanctioned by legitimate authority, that is the state. Cicero argued for right conduct – virtue or courage – in fighting a just war. Consequently, all Rome's external wars against *hostes*, public enemies, especially barbarians, were regarded as just wars.

With the 4th-century recognition of Christianity as the official religion of the empire, Christians shouldered duties as good citizens, encouraged to fight in just wars for the defence of the Christian empire. For the Roman state, religious enemies joined temporal ones as legitimate targets for war: pagan barbarians and religious heretics within the empire who could be equated with traitors. However, no sooner had Christian writers such as Ambrose of Milan (d.397) integrated Christian acceptance of war based on the model of the Israelites with the responsibilities and ideology of Roman citizenship than the political collapse of the empire in the west threatened to undermine the whole theoretical basis of Christian just war. This conundrum was resolved by Augustine of Hippo (d.430) who, in passages scattered unsystematically through his writings, combined Classical and Biblical ideas of holy and just war to produce general principles independent of the Christian/ Roman Empire. To the Helleno-Roman legal idea of right causes and ends, Augustine added a Christian interpretation of moral virtue to right intent and authority. From his diffuse comments three familiar essentials emerged: just cause, defined as defensive or to recover rightful possession; legitimate authority; right intent by participants. Thus war, inherently sinful, could promote righteousness. These attributes form the basis of classic Christian just war theory, as presented, for example, by Thomas Aquinas (1225–74). But Augustine did not regard violence as an ideal, preferring the world of the spirit to that of the flesh. His justification of war looked to the wars of the Old Testament: 'the commandment forbidding killing was not broken by those who have waged war on the authority of God.' Augustine was implicitly moving the justification of violence from lawbooks to liturgies, from the secular to the religious. However, his lack of definition in merging holy and just war, extended in a number of pseudo-Augustinian texts and commentaries, produced a convenient conceptual plasticity that characterized the development of Christian attitudes to war over the subsequent millennium and more. The language of the *bellum justum* became current, while what was often described came closer to *bellum sacrum*. This fusion of ideas might conveniently be called religious war, wars conducted for and by the Church, sharing features of holy and just war, in a protean blend that allowed war to become valid as an expression of Christian vocation second only to monasticism itself.

A just war was not necessarily a holy war, although all holy wars were, *per se*, just. While holy war depended on God's will, constituted a religious act, was directed by clergy or divinely sanctioned rulers, and offered spiritual rewards, just war formed a legal category justified by secular necessity, conduct and aim, attracting temporal benefits. The fusion of the two became characteristic of later Christian formulations. Where Rome survived, in Byzantium, the eastern empire of Constantinople, the coterminous relation of Church and State rendered all public war in some sense holy, in defence of religion, approved by the Church. However, Byzantine warfare remained a secular activity, for all its Divine sanction, not, as it became in late 11th-century western Europe, a penitential act of religious votaries. Elsewhere in Christendom, while the ideals of pacifism remained fiercely defended by the monastic movement and its ideal of the contemplative life, Christians and their Church had to confront new secular attitudes to warfare consequent on political domination by a Christianized Germanic military elite and new external threats from non-Christians.

## New Defenders of the Faith in the early Middle Ages

War occupied a central place in the culture as well as politics of the Germanic successor states to the Roman Empire from the 5th century. The great German historian of the origins of the crusading mentality, Carl Erdmann, argued that for the new rulers of the west war provided 'a form of moral action, a higher type of life than peace'. Heavily engaged in converting these warlords, the Christian Church necessarily had to recognize their values, not least because, with the collapse of Roman civil institutions, economic and social order revolved around the fiscal and human organization of plunder, tribute, and dependent bands of warriors held together by kinship and lordship. Their Gods were tribal deliverers of earthly victory and reward. It has been said that the early medieval army, the *exercitus*, assumed a role as the pivotal public institution in and through which operated justice, patronage, political discipline, diplomacy, and ceremonies of communal identity, usually with the imprimatur of religion, pagan or Christian. The effect of the conversion of these Germanic peoples worked in two directions: the Christianizing of their warrior ethic and the militarizing of the Church.

Contemporary descriptions of the conversion and early Christian kings of the new political order are peppered with martial heroes in the style of Constantine himself, such as Clovis the Frank (d.511) or Oswald of Northumbria (d.644). Conversely, Christian evangelists and holy men were depicted exercising physical aggression as God's agents in the style of the Old Testament Moses. Unsurprisingly, Germanic warrior values infected the language of the faith being conveyed, even if only in the seedbed of metaphor. In the 8th-century Anglo-Saxon *Dream of the Rood*, Christ is depicted as 'the young warrior', 'the Lord of Victories'; death on the cross as a battle, with Heaven a sort of Valhalla. A 9th-century Old German poetic version of the Gospel story shows Christ as a lord of men, 'a generous mead-giver', his disciples a war band travelling in warships, Peter 'the mighty noble swordsman'. While fiercely resisted by many academics and monks, this militarized mentality received the powerful confirmation of events.

The historical as well as literary type of the early medieval warrior was Charlemagne (d.814), king of the Franks and, from 800,

71

emperor of the west, his wars against pagan Saxons and Avars portrayed by eulogists, official propaganda, and the Church in terms of the Faith. Given that forcible conversion acted as part of his policy of subduing the Saxons, the image reflected actual war aims. Through prayers, blessings of warriors and their arms, liturgies, and differential scales of penance, the Frankish Church elevated these conflicts into holy wars. More widely, the Church presided over a political culture in which the figure of the armed warrior increasingly received religious as well as social approbation, a development sharply illustrated in contemporary saints' lives. Warfare came to be recognized as possessing positive moral as well as political value. As with the Roman Empire it professed to be reviving, in the Carolingian Empire of the 8th and 9th centuries, public war was *ipso facto* just and sanctioned by God. This became even more apparent from the mid-9th century when, with the disintegration of Carolingian power, western Europe was beset by new external attacks from Muslims, Vikings, and Magyars which lent an urgent, dynamic quality to the practice as well as theory of Christian warfare. Political and religious survival became synonymous as a concept of a religious community, Christendom (*Christianitas*), replaced the disintegrating political community of the Frankish Empire. Confronted by Muslims threatening Rome itself, Pope John VIII (872–82) offered penitential indulgences remitting the penalties of sin to those who fought and died fighting. His predecessor Leo IV (847–55) had similarly promised salvation to warriors against the infidels. The identification of religion and war surfaced across western Europe. Monkish propagandists invariably called the Danish enemies of Alfred, king of Wessex (871–99), pagans; his commanders decorated their swords with Christian motifs and their battles were accompanied by prayers and alms. A Frankish monastic annalist similarly described Danish attacks as an 'affront not to us but to Him who is all powerful'. Such explicit Christian militancy, designed to inspire resistance and confirm communal solidarity, enlisted some unlikely recruits. Even St Benedict (d.*c*.550), founder of the main contemplative monastic movement of western Europe, was depicted in the later

9th century as fighting the Vikings 'with his left hand directing and shielding the cavalry and with his right killing many enemies with his staff'.

This militarization of western Christian culture that long predated the Crusades should not be exaggerated. The monastic ideal persisted, Aelfric of Cerne, abbot of Eynsham, at the end of the 10th century insisting on the monks' vocation as 'God's champions in the spiritual battle, who fight with prayers not swords; it is they who are the soldiers of Christ'. Although examples of warrior saints, or saints who were once warriors, proliferated in the 10th and 11th centuries, the moral dangers of fighting continued to be recognized. However, at least from Carolingian penitential observances onwards, churchmen drew a distinction between killing in a public conflict authorized by a legitimate secular (or religious) authority, *bellum*, and illicit private war, sometimes distinguished by the word *guerra*, those fighting in the former receiving lighter penances for their killing than those engaged in the latter. Still, the actual act of combat remained sinful; despite fighting under a papal banner in a cause considered by their clergy to be just, William of Normandy's followers in 1066 were forced to perform modest penance for the slaughter they inflicted at the Battle of Hastings. The late 11th-century revolution lay particularly in the settled transformation of the actual violence, rather than its purpose, scale, or intent, into a penitential act.

## The origins of the crusade in the 11th century

The changing articulation of the long-held acceptance of legitimate religious war that combined elements of the Helleno-Roman and Biblical traditions was fashioned as much by political circumstance as by theology. Renewed attention to Augustinian theory from the late 11th century came in response, not as an inspiration, to greater ecclesiastical militancy. Secular influences included the problem of public authority and social order after the collapse of Charlemagne's empire in the 9th and 10th centuries; the altered terms of the frontier conflicts with Islam, with Christians from the 10th century increasingly on the offensive; and a greater ideological and political stridency of the papacy. Behind all of these lay the cultural identity between lay and clerical rulers who belonged to the same propertied aristocracy. Bishops took the field in battles, sometimes in armour, often at the head of their own military entourage, occasionally engaging in physical combat. Equally, many of the most vicious secular lords were patrons of monasteries, went on exhausting and dangerous pilgrimages, and died in monastic habits as associate members of religious orders.

This cultural intimacy, a feature of the whole of the early Middle Ages, took on greater significance in the development of holy war as the apparatus of civil authority devolved downwards nearer to the human and material resources on which all power depended as public authority was usurped by private lordships. Although less anarchic than once imagined, new social conditions by the end of the 10th century encouraged violence as a means of settling disputes as well as achieving more larcenous or territorial ambitions. This fragmentation of power in western Francia (more or less the region from the Rhine to the Pyrenees, later the cradle of the crusade), by negating kingship, resulted in a deficit of effective public arbitration or political discipline. In such circumstances, to secure protection and status, many churchmen deliberately promoted the responsibility of men of violence to protect the church. To achieve this, the activities of the warrior had to receive explicit praise not just on the level of public wars against pagans and heretics. This acceptance of the need for warlike protectors can be traced in saints' lives and monastic chronicles that exhibit a characteristic schizophrenia when tackling the gilded 'faithful to God' who were also self-serving killers, the contrast later favoured by crusade apologetics between *militia* and *malitia*.

The symbiotic relationship of church and local military aristocracies found concrete expression in formal proceedings organized by local or regional clergy to ensure the physical protection and policing of their property. From the late 10th century, across the duchy of Aquitaine and Burgundy, later spreading to northern France and the Rhineland, church councils were convened that proclaimed the Peace of God with arms bearers swearing, in public ceremonies, to protect those outside the military classes, effectively churchmen and their property. From the 1020s specific periods of weeks or months were designated as Truces of God, during which all such violence should cease, again to be policed by sworn warriors. Although some have challenged the direct influence of the Peace and Truce of God on the origins of crusading, the Council of Clermont in 1095 authorized a Peace of God at the same time as initiating the Jerusalem campaign. These local churchmen, often in concert with regional counts, were not simply condemning illicit attacks on their interests but approving, indeed promoting, violence to prevent them. From being called upon to bless wars for causes sacred and profane, the Church now assumed the roles of author and director, its warriors that of religious votaries.

This trend received strong impetus from the 1050s through the concern of successive popes with the idea and practice of holy war as a weapon to establish the independence of the Church from lay control, contest the authority of the German emperor, ensure the political autonomy of the Roman see, and recover the lost lands of Christendom. The moral standing of those who fought for the papal agenda became an important aspect of the general policy, both in the need to attract support and to assert the uniqueness of the cause. In 1053, Leo IX (1048–54), leading an army in person against the Normans of southern Italy, offered German troops remission of penance and absolution for their sins, a tradition followed by his successors. Papal banners were awarded to the Norman invaders of Muslim Sicily (1060) and England (1066) and to the Milanese Patarines, street gangs contesting control of the city against the imperialists in the 1060s and 1070s in a struggle elevated in papal rhetoric to a *bellum Dei*, a war of God. To combat the ecclesiastical power of Emperor Henry IV (1056–1106) in

Germany and his political ambitions in Italy, Pope Gregory VII (1073–85), one of whose favourite quotations was 'Cursed be he that keepeth back his sword from blood' (Jeremiah 48:10), sought to recruit his own army, the *militia Sancti Petri*. Papal apologists began to write of an *ordo pugnatorum*, an order of warriors, who fought 'for their salvation and the common good', very much the target audience identified by Urban II in 1095. By the end of his pontificate, Gregory's rhetoric transformed the status of his warriors, comparing their service in defence of the Church as an imitation of Christ's suffering against 'those who are the enemies of the cross of Christ'. War had become an act of penance. An abortive project for an eastern expedition in 1074 proposed by Gregory VII to aid Byzantium evinced many elements later deployed by Urban II. Gregory referred to the mandate of God and example of Christ; the goal of Jerusalem; help for the eastern church as an act of charity; and the offer of 'eternal reward'. All that was missing were the vow, the cross, and the associated privileges.

The papacy's advocacy of a more embracive theory and practice of holy war mirrored a wider transformation in the religious life of 11th- and 12th-century western Europe from an essentially local and cultish faith, with regional saints and liturgies, to one more regulated by pastoral uniformity, canon law, and international ecclesiastical discipline. Devotion to saints and their relics became increasingly universal, with a concurrent emphasis on the historicity of the gospel stories, the humanity of Christ, and the cult of the Virgin Mary, which began to dominate church dedications across Christendom. Coupled with the development of elaborate Easter rituals featuring Christ's agonies for Man's Redemption and an increased concentration on the Christocentric aspects of the Mass (for example the Real Presence, the use of crucifixes, and so on), the image of the Holy Land, of Christ's suffering, and of Christian obligation penetrated far beyond the reach of papal rhetoric. The increased popularity of international or Biblical saints reflected anxiety over salvation that the new conception of war addressed directly. The perceived celestial clout of saints had long been a factor in their level of popularity, leading to the strenuous promotion of local shrines by their guardians and the reciprocal gifts of alms and property from the faithful. Penance emerged as a most urgent issue for laymen because the methods for laymen to attain remission of the penalties of sin remained rudimentary. The problem may have appeared especially acute for lay arms bearers, paradoxically because their function had come under such close ecclesiastical scrutiny and acceptance. If monastic charters and chronicles can be believed, penitential war answered a genuine craving to expiate sin. The First Crusade drew excited praise as 'a new way of salvation' for the military classes. Apart from donations to monasteries so that monks could pray for their souls, increasingly laymen in the 11th century found pilgrimages promoted by the clergy as a means to expiate sin, with Jerusalem prominent in practice and imagination. Psychologically, if not legally, religious wars, especially against distant targets such as infidels, lent themselves to identification with pilgrimages as both were conducted for God and involved journeys, always a powerful spiritual metaphor. Gregory VII's reference to going on to the Holy Sepulchre in his 1074 plan suggested a fusion of war (to help eastern Christians) and pilgrimage, a connection repeated by Urban II in granting indulgences in 1089 to those colonizing Tarragona on the Muslim frontier in Spain. The Pisans who attacked Mahdia in Tunisia in 1087 fitted in a pilgrimage to Rome. The concept of an armed pilgrimage has frequently been identified as the key to explain the novel appeal of the expedition preached by Urban II, offering a familiar frame for a new secular act of penance.

However, there remain problems with this interpretation of Urban's scheme. On the one hand, armed pilgrimages to Jerusalem pre-dated 1095; at least one group of armed German pilgrims in 1064 also wore crosses. On the other, in his correspondence in 1095–6, Urban avoided any explicit reference to pilgrimage, talking instead of a military expedition (*expeditio*) to 'restrain the savagery of the Saracens by their arms'. The portrayal of the Jerusalem war as a pilgrimage emerged during the recruitment process, possibly from the clergy who had to broadcast the message and articulate crusaders' motives when compiling records of their fundraising. Urban's penitential journey could best be understood canonically as a pilgrimage, with the emphasis on its spiritual quality. The pope's language and many charters were less ambivalent, calling for the violent expulsion of the infidel from the holy places 'to fight for God against pagans and Saracens', as one Burgundian charter put it. Images of infidel atrocity, brutality, and force permeate Urban's letters stressing the legitimacy of the war, both in terms of right authority (the pope's) and right intent ('devotion alone') to counter any unease at such a blatant call to arms. Early responses, such as the Rhineland massacres, indicated the centrality of violence in the enterprise. The current historiographical emphasis on the pious motives of crusaders can obscure the direct relationship between piety and violence that influential elements in the Church had willingly encouraged, recognizing them as mutually engaged mentalities: service to Christ as physical vengeance; the dangers of campaigning as the imitation of Christ's sufferings; war as an act of charity. In addressing a violent society, Urban, a French aristocrat as well as a former monk, did not compromise with its values: he and his ideology were part of it. Charters provide as much evidence for martial as for pious responses to the First Crusade. Even the letters of crusaders on the march are sparing in their association with pilgrimage, although by 1099 and after the link became ubiquitous. As a holy war, transcendent, spiritual, emotive, the Jerusalem journey was rendered special by the plenary indulgences and the elevated goal of the Holy Sepulchre. Given its stated objective – Jerusalem – an armed pilgrimage may have seemed an appropriate analogy to clerical observers, as nervous of unashamed innovation as of unfettered violence. Only by virtue of the Jerusalem journey becoming a habit did it require fitting into the existing structure of devotional exercises. Urban seemed to have conceived of the operation as unique and unrepeatable; he preached it openly as holy war not armed pilgrimage, a new vision of a very old idea.

Western Christianity held no monopoly on holy war. The Byzantine Empire retained the Roman unity of Church and State that allowed all State conflicts to attract ecclesiastical blessing. Greek emperors portrayed themselves as champions of the Church, especially when fighting pagan Slavs in Bulgaria or Muslims in the Near East. While never interfering with practical diplomacy, Byzantine holy war rhetoric could adopt motifs familiar in the west, as in 975 when John I Tzimisces (969–76) invaded Syria and northern Palestine and may have dangled the prospect, if only in his propaganda, of the reconquest of the holy sites of Jerusalem. Byzantine holy war asserted an integral dimension of public policy, while never attracting the association of violence as penance. It lacked the novelty or the political and spiritual autonomous dynamism of its western counterpart, hence the slightly jaded, condescending superiority expressed by Greek observers, such as Anna Comnena (1083–1153), daughter and biographer of Emperor Alexius I, at the enthusiasm of the early crusaders.

By contrast, the Muslim *jihad* has regularly and lazily been compared with western Christian holy war and the crusade. Unlike the crusade, under Islamic law derived from the Koran, *jihad*, struggle, is enjoined on all members of the Muslim community. Unlike the crusade, according to classical Islamic theory traditionally dating from the 7th and 8th centuries but possibly later, the *jihad* takes two forms: the greater (*al-jihad al-akbar*), the internal struggle to achieve personal purity, a concept not too far removed from St Paul's martial metaphors for the spiritual life; and the lesser (*al-jihad al-asghar*), the military struggle against infidels. Both were obligatory on able-bodied Muslims, but while the former existed as a permanent individual obligation, the lesser *jihad* could be interpreted as a communal activity. Unlike the crusade and Christian holy war, to which the Islamic *jihad* appears to have owed nothing (and vice versa), *jihad* was fundamental to the Muslim faith, a sixth pillar. The essence of *jihad* remained as a spiritual exercise. Its operation depended on context. In the Muslim lands, the *Dar al-Islam* (House of Islam), a grudging religious tolerance was guaranteed by early Islamic texts, at least for the People of the Book, Jews and Christians; instead of persecution or enforced conversion they more profitably paid a special poll tax, the *jizya*. *Pace* modern sentimentalists and apologists, there existed little generosity in such tolerance, merely pragmatism. By contrast, beyond Islamic rule, in the *Dar al-harb* (House of War), non-Muslim political structures and individuals were open to attack as, in Koranic theory, the whole world must recognize or embrace Islam (which means surrender, that is to God) through conversion or subjugation. As with Christian holy war, circumstances determined the *mujahiddin* nature and conduct of *jihad* as much as theory. In frontier areas, such as in Spain or Anatolia, groups of *ghazi* or *mujahiddin* holy warriors, flourished as mercenaries, in tribal groups or, as in the military *ribats* of Muslim Spain, in quasi-monastic communities. With the zeal of new converts, the Seljuk Turks gave the *jihad* a new impetus along the border with Byzantium, but for generations before the spiritual revival of the 12th century there was little attention paid within the Muslim Near East to martial as opposed to spiritual *jihad*. It remains a moot point whether the advent of the crusaders or fundamentalist revivalism originating further east excited the new military fanaticism espoused by the 12th-century Zengids and Ayyubids. In later periods, the dominance of the Ottomans and an uncertainty, which persists, about the existence of a genuine *Dar al-Islam*, complicated attitudes to *jihad*. However, the genesis, nature, and implementation of *jihad* cannot be equated directly with those of the crusade; it operated and operates in a very different ideological and religious value system, with different inspirations and justifications, even if its power to inspire and its physical consequences can be equally bloody for its victims and obsessive for its initiates.

## Holy war, crusade, and Christian society after 1095

In medieval Christendom the malleable contingency of the crusade in concept and practice ensured its popularity and longevity. The defined uniqueness of the Jerusalem journey allowed its essentials – the vow, the cross, plenary indulgence, and temporal privileges – to be transferred to other theatres of religious and ecclesiastical conflict on the principle of equivalence: Spain, the Baltic, internal enemies of the papacy, and heretics. The success of 1099 silenced most critics as well as establishing later conduct. Holy war, commanded by God, earning spiritual reward, continued to provide an important weapon in the papacy's armoury. To signal especial gravity (or papal favour), a comparison with the Jerusalem war could be drawn. However, the Jerusalem model exerted only limited influence on canon law and in no sense became the universal or exclusive form of Christian holy war. Its most profound and lasting innovation came with the 12th- and 13th-century creations of military religious orders, embodiments of the oxymoronic nature of Christian holy war, whose members became, uniquely in Christian society, permanent, professional holy warriors. As a holy war, the crusade fell outside the categories for just war explored in detail in the *Decretum* (first redaction *c*.1139, enlarged edition by 1158) traditionally ascribed to Gratian of Bologna, its legal implications deriving from its associated privileges standing apart from both the academic attempts to define and limit warfare and the experience of battles of the cross. Away from the Curia, especially in frontier regions on Christendom's northern and southern borders, where traditions of inter-communal and inter-faith conflicts readily merged, holy war offered a natural recourse, its acceptability parallel to that of crusading, deriving from similar cultural impulses, but not necessarily narrowly determined by the Jerusalem war. The Danish writer Saxo Grammaticus (*c*.1200) carefully cast his heroes in the Danish wars against their neighbours in terms both specifically of crusade and more generally of holy war. For his employer Archbishop Absalom of Lund (d.1202), it was 'no less religious to repulse the enemies of public faith than to uphold its ceremonies'; he was content to make 'an offering to God not of prayers but of arms'. Similarly in Spain, the granting of formal crusading privileges acted within a context of growing identification of the Reconquista with holy war; as early as *c.*1115, the patron saint, the Apostle St James, was described in a northern Spanish chronicle as 'the knight of Christ'.

While the long tradition of holy war continued to supply the emotional intensity for a range of Christian warfare, the Jerusalem war and its derivatives did not escape the scrutiny of lawyers and academics who increasingly sought to integrate the crusade into a comprehensive canonical justification for violence, rather than, as the appeals for the First and Second Crusades implied, rely simply on Divine mandate and the individual devotional standards of participants. Until the 13th century, and arguably beyond, the crusade remained an ill-defined legal concept. Where Christian war coincided with classical just war categories, as with the defence of Outremer ('the heritage of Christ'), national defence, or the suppression of heretics, fusion with classical and Augustinian just war appeared obvious. In the temporal sphere, it also became necessary, in clerical eyes, to produce a detailed set of legal conditions determining the validity of warfare as crusade targets diversified around 1200, at the same time as secular attitudes to violence coalesced into social norms manifested in the cult of 'chivalry'. The more respectable war became, the more urgent the need for the Church to define what was and what was not sinful about it, especially as Innocent III and his successors transformed crusading into a universal Christian obligation involving all society. Thus, as an aspect of the pastoral reformation within the western church, holy war, not specifically crusading, became tempered by theories of the just war, so much so that the mid-13th-century canonist Hostiensis came close to defining a crusade simply as a papally authorized just war. By the end of the 14th century, Honoré Bonet (or Bouvet) in the *Tree of Battles* (1387) answered the question 'By what law or on what ground can war be made against the Saracens?' with wholly traditional arguments based solely on a just cause – occupation of Christian land or rebellion against Christian rule, and papal authority. In this fashion, the crusade had become reintegrated into a characteristic western European concept of legitimate violence, catching its inspiration from holy war and its legality, rules, and restraints, if any, from classical just war theory. As such the language, motifs, and institutions of crusading penetrated into conflicts where no formal apparatus of crusading existed, for example the adoption of crosses by national armies, such as the Danes *c.*1200 or the English in the 14th century. So pervasive were the symbols and habits of crusading that they could be turned to any political conflict that boasted an ideological tinge, even in the most contradictory of circumstances. Crosses were offered enemies of papal crusaders in southern Germany in 1240. During his rising against what he saw as the misgovernment of Henry III of England in 1263–5, Simon de Montfort's rebels donned the white crusader crosses of the English kings, traditional since the Third Crusade, to fight royalist crusaders. The prominence lent holy war by the Crusades contributed to the familiar western European habit of warring parties of more or less whatever description invoking self-righteous religiosity in support of their cause, a habit, exported to European settlements around the world from the 17th century, that remains current in the 21st century.

Whatever its legal frame, crusading operated as the ultimate manifestation of conviction politics in medieval western Europe, entrenching a narrow cultural and religious exclusivity. When crusaders sacked Lisbon in October 1147, they murdered the local Mozarab Christian bishop alongside his fellow Arabic-speaking Muslim neighbours before happily installing an Englishman, Gilbert of Hastings, as the new bishop. The failure of the Latin Church hierarchy easily to cooperate or combine with higher ranks of the eastern churches in Outremer or, later, Greece was notorious. Although inherent in all holy wars, demonization of opponents reached extreme levels in crusading rhetoric, reflecting both a literary genre and a worldview conducive to a siege mentality, a form of cultural paranoia so often the underbelly of cultural assertiveness. Racism and intolerance of minorities were not caused by the Crusades. Indeed, both in the Baltic and Spain, legal, linguistic, cultural, and blood racism deepened in the centuries

14. The medieval ideal of the crusader knight. An English illustration from a mid-13th-century psalter: piety and power.

*after* the main conquest by warriors of the cross. Yet, in anti-Jewish pogroms and wars against heretics and dissent, crusading helped define a rancid aspect of a persecuting mentality that came as the almost inevitable concomitant of a Church bent on supremacy and uniformity to secure its pastoral ends and secular rulers eager for ideological sanction for their wars.

As holy war addressed fundamental issues of Christian identity and, it was frequently proclaimed, Christian survival, its elements remained embedded in European society as well as providing a cutting edge in the expansion of Latin Christendom southwards, eastwards, and northwards. The habit of crusading died hard; in the 15th century crusading formulae were natural appendages for the expansion of European power down the west coast of Africa and into the eastern Atlantic, as they were in the religious wars in Bohemia as well as in defence against the Turks. In the 16th century and beyond, the Ottomans kept the images and occasionally the reality of the war of the cross alive, while the internal religious divisions in Europe ushered in a period of religious wars no less vicious in commitment and butchery than anything witnessed in previous centuries. Some historians would argue that the period of the Crusades defined Christianity's affection for holy war – far from it. The Crusades formed only one articulation of Christian holy war, whose origins long pre-dated 1095 and whose legacy refused to fade. Even in a supposedly more secular age, self-righteous, ideologically justified warfare persists. The modern world has embraced, variously with horror and energy, ideological, religious, and pseudo-religious violence as well as racist, nationalist, and anti-Semitic pogroms on an industrial scale, all in the context of justifying moralities. The moral high ground of the 21st century, whether shaded by the banners of religion, reason, capitalism, or freedom, still lies pitted with the rank shell-holes of holy war.

# Chapter 6
# The business of the cross

Crusading was not a spontaneous act. An individual rush of
conviction or the sudden collective convulsion of a crowd might
provoke the initial act of commitment, the adoption of the cross.
However, the translation of that obligation into action depended on
personal, political, social, financial, and economic preparation and
planning and generated widely diffused legal and fiscal institutions.
No cross, no crusade, but equally no money, no crusade; no group,
no crusade; no leadership, no crusade; no transport, no crusade. If
this sounds reductive, it is. Piety and what may pass for religious
energy contribute to an explanation of motive and campaign
morale. Armies may march on their stomachs, but it is difficult to
make them fight and die without a cause, without some internal
dynamic that acts beyond reason to send warriors over the top or
stand their ground. But all the passion in the universe could not,
cannot, create war, crusading or not, without the organization and
manipulation of recruitment, finance, logistics, military structure –
and ideas.

## Preaching

Preaching demonstrates this, providing some of crusading's most
familiar images. A preacher, arriving in a town or village bearing
a tale of disaster, a call to battle, a promise of salvation, and a
knapsack of crosses, converts his audience by his fervour and

15. Bernard of Clairvaux preaching the Second Crusade at Vézelay, Easter 1146. This romantic vision, by E. Signol, was displayed in the Salles des Croisades at Versailles in 1838 and owes everything to imagination rather than fact.

eloquence alone. Urban II at Clermont provided the prototype, Christ and John the Baptist the imagined models. Such scenes punctuate crusade history: the inspirational Bernard of Clairvaux on the hillside at Vézelay in 1146; the prosaic Archbishop Baldwin of Canterbury stomping around Wales in 1188; the charismatic Fulk of Neuilly stirring up northern France around 1200; the sophisticated James of Vitry beguiling the rich women of Genoa in 1216. Yet preaching worked within tightly organized programmes of information and recruitment in which the sermon provided only a focus. Chroniclers and the preachers themselves idealized the process into a perfect system of evangelism which engaged the faithful directly with the orthodox teaching of the Church, as well as supplying a useful starting point for a didactic narrative. In a semi-literate society, ceremonial rituals, of which the crusade sermon was one of the most conspicuous, provided a powerful medium for conveying public messages. However, to achieve any effect, the significance of such rituals needed to be understood beforehand, either by long use, as with the Latin Mass, prior publicity, or rehearsal. The crusade preacher expected to preach, if not to the converted, then to the prepared whose interest needed confirmation through a series of formulaic responses, most obviously the taking of the cross. Along with their supply of cloth crosses to be given to the *crucesignati*, crusade preachers armed themselves with rolls of parchment on which to write the names of the recruits. Without good preparation, the whole procedure could fall flat; in 1267, when Louis IX took the cross for the second time, apparently many refused to follow his example because they had not been warned what was afoot.

Evidence for crusade sermons before the late 12th century remains dependent on chronicle accounts. From these it appears such sermons were neither regular nor widespread before the Third Crusade. With the rise in the use of crusading as a military weapon and its integration into the wider devotional life of the Christian west, the frequency of crusade preaching increased and its organization by the papacy became more systematic. Innocent III used Cistercians for the Fourth Crusade and a corps of Paris trained reformers such as James of Vitry for the Albigensian and Fifth Crusades. From the 1230s his successors employed the Friars as the main crusade proselytizers. Paradoxically, after Innocent III's bull *Quia Maior* (1213) for the Fifth Crusade, the frequency of sermons operated in inverse proportion to their role in recruitment as the offer of the uniquely redemptive plenary crusade indulgence was extended to non-combatants. Crusade preaching increasingly acted as part of more general evangelizing. Still promoting a particular spiritual endeavour and commitment, the function of sermons broadened to include fundraising as well as recruitment.

Crusade sermons followed patterns of form and presentation to ensure the outcome peculiar to this particular ritual, the physical commitment of taking the cross. As at modern evangelical and revivalist meetings, the congregation could not remain passive. They had to 'come on down' and, therefore, needed to be primed by example and expectation. All rituals need careful stage-management if they are to convey meaning and avoid absurdity and the disbelief of the audience – crusade sermons, with their layers of intent and lack of regularity, more than most. At Clermont, Urban II was careful to ensure that, once he had finished speaking, Adhemar, bishop of Le Puy, immediately came forward to show the rest of the congregation how to take the cross, while a cardinal in the back row set up the chant of 'God wills it!' as a means of inspiring a sense of group involvement. Neither Clermont nor any of the other assemblies that witnessed the great arias of crusade rhetoric over the next five centuries gathered by chance, but by careful arrangement. In 1146, no accident had brought together the nobility of France to hear Bernard of Clairvaux at Vézelay; he had brought with him 'a parcel of crosses which had been prepared beforehand'. Louis VII, sitting on the platform beside Bernard, had voiced his interest in the Holy Land campaign months before, and was already wearing a cross sent him by the pope, leaving no doubt as to the purpose of the occasion. Bernard's task was to publicize the papal bull, explaining the need for war and the spiritual and temporal privileges, and to confirm recruits. His sermons in 1146–7 merely highlighted the issues and secured previously agreed responses. This became the usual form. When Archbishop Baldwin toured Wales in Lent 1188, his audiences knew in advance exactly when and where to meet him and what to do. At Basel in 1201, the crowds flocking to hear Abbot Martin of Pairis's formulaic, if apparently moving, address had been 'stimulated by rumours' of crusade preaching and arrived 'prepared in their hearts to enlist in Christ's camp . . . hungrily anticipating an exhortation of this sort'. Yet the author of this account went out his way, despite his own testimony, to portray Martin's sermon as autonomously inspirational.

A whole gallery of manipulative techniques was employed to support the rhetoric. Props included relics of the True Cross, crucifixes, and visual aids. A Muslim contemporary described how preachers of the Third Crusade in 1188 travelled around with a large illustrated canvas. On it, a Muslim cavalryman was depicted trampling the Holy Sepulchre, on which his horse had urinated. While, by the 13th century, congregations had grown familiar with special prayers and processions dedicated to the Holy Land as well as ceremonies for taking the cross, there were still no liturgical formularies for responses to sermons. In this ritual of penance and commitment, the congregation needed direction. One aid was provided by the seasons of the church calendar, crusade sermons often being delivered during the penitential seasons of Lent or Advent, or at the great Christocentric festivals of Easter and Christmas, or on 14 September, Holy Cross Day. Another came from a telling liturgical setting, frequently the Mass with its concentration on the physicality of the Body and Blood of Christ. Audiences were softened up and involved by the use of chants and slogans – football crowds meet Billy Graham in religious circus. When Cardinal Henry of Albano preached in Germany in 1188, the clergy and laity sang hymns about Jerusalem to get everyone into the mood. Once signed up, *crucesignati* sang songs or chants to encourage corporate identity, or recited together the General

Confession from the Mass to underline the penitential nature of their undertaking. Getting audiences to that point was not left to chance or oratory alone. James of Vitry observed that to encourage others it helped to have a member of the audience come forward promptly to take the cross at the end of the sermon, to break the ice, and, like Adhemar of Le Puy at Clermont, show how it was done. At Radnor in March 1188, Gerald of Wales, having been told by Archbishop Baldwin, the Chief Justiciar of England, and King Henry II himself to set the requisite example (the primate not being the world's most inspirational evangelist), stood up first to take the cross: 'In doing so I gave strong encouragement to the others and an added incentive to what they had just been told.' According to admiring written accounts, crusade preaching campaigns were accompanied by sightings of miracles, sometimes as simple as clouds shaped in the beholders' eye as crosses or other celestial portents, natural accompaniment to such overt religious exercises. The whole operation rested on calculation, planning, and showmanship.

The content of sermons functioned within this highly artificial, ritualized staging. Often using the relevant papal bull, preachers rehearsed past events and explained the justification for war both on the grounds of atrocities to be avenged and of moral duty. A common literary and possibly genuine experience described how the emotions not the actual words preached were understood, the message reaching the uncomprehending audience by divine rather than oral or aural mediation. The preacher and his words, especially if delivered in Latin to large crowds, were distant, inaudible, or unintelligible as means of direct communication, rather like William Gladstone at his mass meetings in the late 19th century. The occasion was as important as any words. Medieval sermons provided witnesses to divine mystery, settings for spiritual, political, or social dialogue. In the 13th century, to signal this religious ceremonial function, those attending sermons were offered indulgences of their own whether or not they took the cross. Such sermons ritualized enthusiasm rather than rousing rabbles.

Repeated references to interpreters, the survival of morally edifying vernacular anecdotes (*exempla*), and the advice contained in increasingly popular 13th-century preaching manuals suggest that attempts were made to communicate in audiences' own languages as well as Latin. While the sermons that have been preserved tend towards the elaborate and the academic, some preaching veterans emphasized the need for simplicity; others indicated the importance of oratorical tricks, including repetition of almost mantra-like phrases or the inclusion of arresting moral stories variously to illustrate duty, adventure, or salvation.

In combining symbolic spiritual commitment with public church evangelism, crusade sermons represented much of the new reformist idealism associated with the pontificate of Innocent III. Preachers began to think of taking the cross as a form of conversion, a complete amendment of spiritual life similar, if less permanent, to becoming a monk. The crusade sermon's mixture of direct appeal to the laity, penance, confession, and duty to Christ touched most of the key elements of the reformers' programme. Yet these ceremonies also served as key moments in political processes such as the pacification of kingdoms. Monarchs could find in them occasions to confirm their status and elicit open demonstrations of support from their nobles, as did Louis VII of France at Vézelay, Easter 1146; Conrad III of Germany at Speyer, Christmas 1146; and Frederick I of Germany at the so-called 'Court of Christ' at Mainz, where he took the cross in March 1188. At the conference between Philip II of France and Henry II of England at Gisors in January 1188, the need to unite to recover the Holy Land eased the reconciliation of suspicious rivals. Diplomatic compromise could both be sealed and disguised under the banner of the cross. However, whether as an expression of evangelism or diplomacy, or simply a means of raising men and money, the crusade sermon, for all its prominence, performed a series of roles largely subsidiary to the wider organization of crusading. Recruitment followed patterns established beyond the preachers' congregations; locally, ceremonies for taking the cross existed independently. Nonetheless, sermons orchestrated a measure of discipline, of people, responses, and ideas, increasingly attractive to a Church ever more intent on uniformity of belief and devotional practice.

## Recruitment and finance

Crusading armies, like any other, were assembled through a mixture of loyalty, incentive, and cash, and maintained and run through ties of lordship, clientage, sworn association, or, for defaulters, legal coercion. In the absence of kings as clear overlords, for example on the First and Fourth Crusades, these mechanisms proved vital in producing coherence and order. Recruitment revolved around the households and affinities of princes, lords, knights, and urban elites. The misnamed Peasants' Crusade of Peter the Hermit in 1096 differed from other major expeditions only in the social standing of its leaders and the ratio of knights to infantry and, perhaps, non-combatants. In a society in which in many regions the bulk of the population were bound to landlords by servile tenure, only freemen could legitimately take the cross; serfs who did so were *ipso facto* manumitted. On campaign, if no previous bond of allegiance existed, crusaders made their own. Peter the Hermit's expedition in 1096 possessed a common treasury. By the time the Christian host reached Antioch in 1097–8, a joint command had been formed by the leaders of the different contingents with a common fund that channelled money through a sworn confraternity towards essential construction work for the siege. Loyalties could be bought, knights and lords transferring allegiance when they or their own lords died, deserted, or went bust. Even with the involvement of kings, as in the Second and Third Crusades, individual lords remained responsible for their own followers, whether subsidized by monarchs or not.

When lordship threatened to collapse or no clear order of precedence existed, crusaders, like their contemporaries in towns across Europe, resorted to sworn associations known as communes. These established procedures for making decisions, settling disputes, dividing spoils, and imposing discipline. This decidedly non-feudal system of self-government became a crusade commonplace, from the disparate North Sea fleet that assembled at Dartmouth in May 1147 and later helped capture Lisbon, to individual ships' companies from northern European cities in the Third Crusade, to the leadership of the Fourth Crusade. One of the failures of the Fifth Crusade at Damietta lay in its inability to establish either an agreed leader or a sworn commune. Such associations also operated, at least in some corners of France in 1147, at the level of local seigneurial bands coming together to embark on the Lord's business. Sometimes these arrangements failed. The rules sworn by Louis VII and his captains before leaving France in 1147 on the Second Crusade were ignored. Months later, to save the French army from annihilation in Asia Minor, another sworn commune was formed, this time to accept the leadership and discipline of the Templars. Communal leadership did not preclude the military requirement for a clear command structure. The election of Simon de Montfort as commander of the Albigensian Crusade in 1209 saved it from degenerating into a brief foray of rampage and pillage.

The importance of access to finance cannot be overestimated. The commonest reason given by backsliders in England around 1200 for non-fulfilment of the vow was poverty. It is no accident that rules for borrowing money figure prominently in the earliest crusade bull, *Quantum praedecessores* (1145/6) and its most important successors, *Audita Tremendi* (1187) and *Quia Maior* (1213). Much of the evidence for the identity and circumstances of individual crusaders derives from their land deals to raise cash from their landed estates and property, usually from the Church. The cost of crusading represented many times a landowner's annual income. The need for money determined the agreement of the First Crusade leadership in 1097 to swear fealty to the Byzantine emperor. It provided the impetus for the diversion of the Fourth Crusade to Zara (1202) and Constantinople (1203–4). Money allowed Richard I to dominate the Palestine war of 1191–2 on the Third Crusade, and Cardinal Pelagius, through his control of the funds raised by

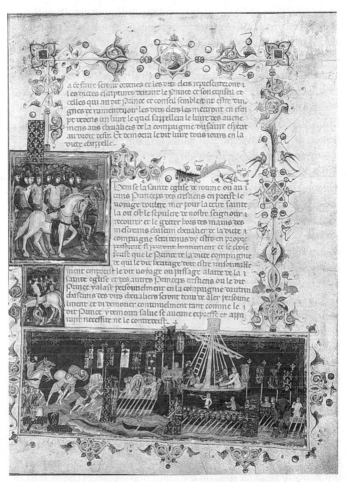

**16.** Preparations for the crusade. From the Statutes of the 14th-century French chivalric Order of the Holy Spirit enjoining on members the obligation to enlist in any crusade to the Holy Land, illustrations emphasizing the essential material dimensions of such enterprises.

taxation of the church in the west, to influence decisions at
Damietta during the Fifth Crusade in 1219–21. Although foraging
allowed land armies to subsist, chroniclers repeatedly exclaimed
at the iniquities of local markets and exorbitant prices from the
Balkans to Syria. For sea transport, the capital outlay could be huge.
During the Third Crusade, Philip II's promise to the Genoese of
5,850 silver marks to ship his army to the Holy Land in 1190
appears extremely modest compared with Richard I's expenditure –
in advance – of £14,000 (c.21,000 marks) on his large fleet alone.
Small wonder Richard felt the need to extort 40,000 gold ounces
from Tancred of Sicily in the winter of 1190–1. The Fourth Crusade
leadership's massive commitment of 85,000 marks to Venice
constituted almost literally a king's ransom (Richard I's came to
100,000 marks in 1194) but paled before Louis IX's estimated
expenditure on his first crusade of 1.5 million *livres tournois*, six
times his annual income.

Talk of money throws up the two old chestnuts of profit and
younger sons. Crusading was very expensive. Without royal or
ecclesiastical subsidies, money had to be raised through selling or
mortgaging property, often at high hidden rates of interest. One
cliché of medieval history insists that people sought to increase
their property at any opportunity, except, it seems, crusaders who
condemned their families at the very least to a short-term and
possibly permanent loss. Given that most crusaders desired, if not
expected, to return, having little interest in permanent emigration,
it is hard to identify where crude material profit in the modern
sense featured in their motives, contenting themselves with the
seemingly no less real rewards of relics, salvation, and social status.

This distinction between crusaders and settlers operates even more
sharply when considering the idea that crusading appealed
especially to younger sons on the make, forced out of the west by the
spread of patrilinear inheritance rules that left only the eldest
holding the inheritance. While it is feasible that settlers, in Syria
but perhaps especially in the Baltic regions, were encouraged to

migrate by lack of prospects at home, this cannot be shown for crusaders. The need for finance meant that armies were manned by those in possession or expectation of patrimonies or those, such as the large number of artisans recorded in crusade forces, who had marketable skills. The foot soldiers were legally but not necessarily economically free. The sources show that crusading ran in propertied families without distinction of inheritance claims, eldest sons, great lords as well as younger siblings and dependent relatives. Emigration, at least amongst aristocrats, may show a tendency to favour those lacking great expectations at home, but this must remain no more than a plausible guess given the inadequate statistical base available of known individual immigrants to Syria, Iberia, or the Baltic. The idea that western inheritance customs, either by excessive partibility of estates or the exclusion of younger sons, explain the 12th- and 13th-century diaspora from the central regions of early medieval Europe – Italy, France, Germany, England – to the Celtic, Slavic, Finno-Ugrian, Greek, or Arabic peripheries may be attractive as a mechanistic model of causation. But evidence suggests it cannot explain the particular phenomenon of crusading where the crusaders were not settlers by intent or even accident. The assumption prevalent until recently that most of the immigration into Frankish Outremer came from the crusade armies no longer looks either credible or accurate; it was never advanced for settlement in Iberia or the Baltic when civilian settlement followed military conquest. Although they individually existed, as general defining types, the mercenary crusader and the younger son must ride into the sunset of serious historical debate together.

In any case, changes in crusade funding in the 13th century transformed the whole basis of participation and organization. Increasingly configured as an obligation on all Christendom, in theory the business of the cross could demand contributions from all the faithful. However, this principle only translated into reality with the development of secular and ecclesiastical political control and fiscal exploitation. Taxation for crusading was introduced only fitfully. To pay for Duke Robert of Normandy's crusade in 1096, his brother King William II Rufus of England levied a heavy land tax in England to pay the 10,000 marks to mortgage the duchy for three years. In 1146–7, Louis VII of France raised money from the church and perhaps from towns in the royal demesne. In response to diplomatic pressure, in 1166 and 1185 the kings of England and France imposed general but modest taxes (of between 1 and 0.4 per cent) on revenues, property, and movables (that is, profits). The defeat at Hattin and loss of Jerusalem in 1187 prompted the radical innovation of the Saladin tithe of 1188 in England and France, a tenth on movables payable by non-*crucesignati*. Once again left to secular rulers to collect, Henry II, always keen to try new forms of financial exaction, met with some success, while opposition forced Philip II to cancel collection in 1189. In Germany, where no tradition of direct royal taxation survived, no such levy was instituted. Although it is unclear how much money Henry II raised from the Saladin tithe, still less how much was actually spent on the crusade, the form of the tax provided a model for consensual and parliamentary grants in the following century. However, taxation operated by secular powers was subject to the vagaries of secular politics and custom. In France, the obligation to pay for a lord's crusade joined the three traditional feudal aids of ransom, knighting of the eldest son, and marriage of the eldest daughter. In England, government crusade taxation only surfaced when the holy business became central royal policies, as in the years leading to the Lord Edward's crusade of 1271–2, which elicited a parliamentary grant in 1270. In France in the 1240s, Louis IX similarly channelled large sums from royal revenues towards the crusade.

However, Louis IX did not have to rely on his own resources; two-thirds of his estimated expenses came from a grant of church taxation. The raising of money directly from ecclesiastical revenues by the church authorities themselves revolutionized crusade funding. First instituted, unsuccessfully, by Innocent III in 1199, after the decree *Ad Liberandam* of the Fourth Lateran Council in 1215 approving a grant of one-twentieth of church income for three years for the Fifth Crusade, all subsequent major crusade enterprises sought similar ecclesiastical taxes, often to the dismay of local church leaders. Such institutionalized fiscal incorporation of the church into crusading operations matched the newly articulated ideology of universal involvement of Christendom in the Lord's War. Beside ecclesiastical taxation, mechanisms were developed between 1187 and 1215 that allowed pious laymen to donate funds for the crusade on a more or less permanent basis through charitable giving (gifts and alms), legacies, and, from 1213, vow redemptions. Far from signalling mercenary exploitation of a corrupt ideal, as some historians have argued, the offer of cash redemption of crusade vows in return for crusade indulgences mirrored the Church's attempts to evangelize the laity through a wider range of penitential exercises, on a par with the adoption of compulsory aural confession in 1215. Chests designated for crusade donations appeared in parish churches across Christendom and preachers increasingly sought to promote cash vow redemptions, a move that aroused healthy cynicism among some observers when the task became the preserve of the supposedly mendicant Friars. By the 14th century, crusade indulgences were beginning to be sold outright, without the need to take the cross. Such moves widened the social embrace of crusading and its indulgence to include the old, the infirm, the less well-to-do, and women. The funds from taxation, donations, legacies, and redemptions were gathered by local collectors and administered by the Church, creating a series of cash deposits eagerly sought by aspiring crusaders. Much of the practical business of the cross after 1215 revolved around the management and disposal of these ecclesiastically generated or held funds that directly affected how crusades to the east in particular were recruited.

Sea transport and independent Church funding prompted a more professional approach in assembling armies, with written contracts and cash retainers playing a more evident role. Thus, in 1221, Cardinal Ugolino of Ostia, later Pope Gregory IX (1227–41), toured northern Italy signing onto the Church's payroll crusade recruits who had not taken the cross. Contracts between crusaders specifying payment for a set number of soldiers survive from the 1240s. Richard of Cornwall hoped to pay for much of his crusade in 1240–1 from the proceeds of vow redemptions. Edward of England's crusade of 1271–2, paid for from lay and clerical subsidies, has been described as 'perhaps the first English military force to be systematically organised by the use of written contracts, with standard terms available for service'. The cohesion central funding could provide can be illustrated by the contrasting fates of two of the best-equipped expeditions to the east, Frederick of Germany's of 1189 and Louis IX's of 1249. Frederick's followers had to pay for themselves; after he drowned in 1190 the force disintegrated. Louis IX spent much time both before leaving France in 1248 and throughout the campaign of 1249–50 trying to entice nobles who were not his vassals, like the chronicler John of Joinville, into his paid service. Even after the debacle in the Nile Delta in 1250, Louis's resources held his shattered army together. Ironically, more efficient exploitation of resources reflected increased central control in many kingdoms of the west, which ultimately impeded the crusade by elevating national or dynastic self-interest above international stability. It also altered perceptions of how crusading should best be conducted. The early 14th-century Venetian Marino Sanudo, in advice never actually implemented, argued that any initial attacks of Mamluk Egypt should be undertaken by forces paid from central church funds and manned by professionals, and explicitly *not* by *crucesignati*. This, he felt, would ensure a more efficient military outcome.

An alternative institutional method of funding and recruitment reached its apogee and nadir in the century after 1215. The Military Orders had long offered a source of permanent manpower, with a constant pool of money from their estates in the west. From the 1130s, the Orders had received lavish donations of land and property from pious donors, the profits of which subsidized their activities in the Holy Land and elsewhere. Increasingly, they took over the defence of the Latin states of Outremer and acted as bankers for visiting crusaders. In Spain, strategic frontier defences were entrusted to local as well as international orders. In the Baltic, Military Orders offered the solution to the sporadic, transient, and underfunded lay crusading, with the Teutonic Knights creating their own states in Prussia and Livonia. However, the evacuation of the Holy Land in 1291 led to a widespread soul-searching about the Orders' role and use of their extensive wealth. This debate contributed directly to the persecution and suppression of the Templars between 1307 and 1314 on trumped-up charges of heresy, corruption, and sodomy, as well as to the relocation of the headquarters of the Teutonic Knights at Marienberg in 1309 and the Hospitallers' conquest of Rhodes the same year. Yet many still regarded a combination of general church subsidy with the model of a Military Order, with its channels of funding and structures of command, commitment, and discipline, as potentially the most effective way of organizing a new eastern crusade. However, the very techniques that made such theories possible militated against their fulfilment. Church taxes or the lands of discredited Military Orders were far too lucrative for national governments to leave for the business of the cross that had inspired them.

## The crusade and Christian society

Crusading was a function of western European society. Assessment of its impact must distinguish between the distinctive and the contingent. The wars of the cross did not create the expansion of Latin Christendom or the internationalization of saints' cults. Nor did they create Christianity's embrace of holy war, a more sophisticated penitential system, the birth of purgatory, the militancy of the papal monarchy, the rise in anti-Semitism, or the exclusion or persecution of minorities and Christian dissidents. Unlike the campaigns in the eastern Mediterranean, the conquests and colonization in Spain or the Baltic and the papal wars against its enemies did not owe their inception to crusading formulae. Most people did not go on crusade. Only occasionally could crusading enterprises be regarded as 'popular' in the sense of being initiated primarily by groups below the rural and urban elites, such as the Children's Crusade of 1212 and the Shepherds' Crusades of 1251 and 1320. The wider social involvement came from large-scale recruitment by the nobility in limited areas for specific campaigns and, increasingly, through taxation, the legal implications of the taking of the cross and the extension of access to the indulgence via contributions and vow redemptions after 1200. The concept of 'Crusading Europe' misleads. Nevertheless, these wars added a particular quality to society in their rhetorical definition of a pathology of respectable violence, the unique attraction of the associated privileges, and the disruption to public and private life.

The peculiar fashioning of a vocabulary and practice of penitential violence that developed in the century and a half after 1095 provided the Church with a powerful weapon to aim at its opponents and a means to cement its importance in the politics of its allies and the lives of the faithful. As an activity that justified the social mores of the ruling military elites of the west, crusading became the context for a wide range of unconnected social and political rituals. Landowners dated their charters from their crusading deeds. Diplomatic alliances were agreed under the cloak of aiding the Holy Land. Taking the cross acted as a symbol of reconciliation between parties in dispute or a demonstration of loyalty and allegiance in which no side lost face. Politicians at a low ebb sought help in the language of the cross; King John of England took the cross in 1215 shortly before being forced to agree to the Magna Carta. By the mid-13th century, commitment to the business of the cross had become a requisite in diplomatic exchanges, rulers, such as Henry III of England, who left their vows unfulfilled cutting morally ambiguous figures. Those refusing to go on crusade were popularly known as 'ashy', tied to their home fires. The familiar literary stereotype of the *descroisié*, content to enjoy his crusade privileges through vow redemptions, frightened of the sea, and anxious to protect his position at home, indicated how far crusading institutions had penetrated beyond the recruiting hall.

The social and economic disruption of active crusading varied. The expeditions east of Theobald of Champagne or Richard of Cornwall in 1239–41 did not compare with the great efforts of 1146–8, 1189–92, or 1248–50, while crusades in Spain and the Baltic added only marginal lustre and perhaps some recruits to the habitual campaigning of the Iberian, Danish, or German princes. Yet even small-scale enterprises could influence local land markets and regional balances of wealth and power as crusaders mortgaged or sold their property. For families, the cost of crusading and the absence of property owners for very long periods could be highly damaging, leading to disparagement of estates and widows, or worse, some wives being murdered by impatient claimants to the crusaders' lands. Casualty rates, especially on the land-based expeditions, could be extreme; perhaps over 80% of those who set out in 1096–7 did not survive. Enhanced social standing for returning crusaders may have been little compensation. More generally, the liberation of church-held bullion to subsidize crusaders may have encouraged the circulation of wealth and thus stimulated local economies. Regionally, prices of war commodities, such as horse shoes, arrows, sides of bacon, and cheese could rise, as they did in England in the early 1190s. Suppliers of transport, from mules and carts to the great transmarine fleets, benefited. However, a fair proportion of the wealth collected in the west was dissipated unproductively on war materials and campaign expenses far from home. Crusade taxation, like any other in the Middle Ages, tended to be regressive, falling on those at the base of the economy. That helped to ensure the popularity among aristocratic crusaders of the new financing arrangements in the 13th century. Vow redemptions cost less than active crusading but acted as a hidden tax on the faithful. Yet, without crusading, it cannot be clear that this wealth would have been redirected to more ostensibly productive ends or even circulated at all. International trade between the eastern and western Mediterranean piggy-backed on the Crusades and vice versa; they were manifestations of a single, if diverse, process of commercial expansion of markets and trade routes. An overall financial balance sheet is impossible to determine, but the Crusades, however wasteful of lives and effort, of themselves neither significantly ruined nor enriched the economy of western Europe.

The legal privileges granted crusaders reached as far as finance into the interstices of social life. Church protection and immunity from interest, debts, and law suits were enforced by secular as well as ecclesiastical courts from the Papal Curia downwards. Away from the high-profile cases of infringement of the rules, as when Richard I's lands were threatened in his absence, the operation of the privileges and church protection was conducted in local courts across Christendom, whose decisions defined and determined much of the effect of the crusade on the home front, from whether or not a crusader could participate in a trial by battle in Normandy, to illegal wine-sellers avoiding fines in Worcestershire by citing their crusader status, to whether *crucesignati* could literally get away with murder. The civil attractions of the crusader privileges made abuse inevitable, a problem recognized by the decree *Ad Liberandam* (1215). There were regular complaints that crusaders were using their status as licence to commit theft, murder, and rape; criminals or those facing awkward litigation regularly cited crusade privileges to delay or avoid the day of reckoning. This did not mean the system was corrupt, merely open to corruption. References to the operation of crusading immunities in the records of secular courts allow a glimpse of the extent of the Crusades' reach. They also point to a high level of cooperation between civil and ecclesiastical jurisdictions, not least because there were so few detailed rules, the practical implications and extent of privileges being worked out over many generations on a national, regional, local, or even individual basis.

With the institution of vow redemptions and spiritual rewards for contributing as well as participating in crusading, and the paraphernalia of alms-giving, special prayers, liturgies, processions, and bell-ringing that developed after 1187, the spiritual privileges entered the habitual devotional life of the west. Church reformers saw in the dissemination of its indulgence the opportunity to use the crusade as a model as well as a metaphor for spiritual and penitential amendment of life. Taking the cross became depicted as part of a regenerative cycle of confession, penance, good works, and redemption, a sort of conversion, its votaries described by James of Vitry as a *religio*, a religious order. Some argued that taking the cross could end demonic possession, secure time off purgatory for relatives, even dead ones, cure the sick, and console the dying. Sermons *de Cruce*, on the Cross, were used almost interchangeably for preaching the crusade or moral reform. For devout 13th-century puritans such as Louis IX or Simon de Montfort, the crusade formed part of their private religious life as well as their public career. Thus as a religious habit as much as a martial endeavour, crusading survived its defeats on the battlefields of the later Middle Ages.

This does not imply universal or consistent commitment. The myriad sermons and devotional works reminding the faithful of some basic tenets of Christianity, among other evidence, suggest that the Middle Ages were no more or less a period of faith or scepticism than the 21st century. Contemporaries were as keen to delineate contrasting crusade motives as modern historians. Much of the typology was equally crude. After the fiasco of the Second Crusade, one bitter observer in Würzburg accused the crusaders of lack of sincere love of God; most 'lusted after novelties and went in order to learn about new lands' or out of a mercenary desire to escape poverty, debts, harsh landlords, or justice. Such brickbats are the price of failure and the small change of moral rearmers. The idea that crusaders to the east were driven by greed is considerably less convincing than that they were fired by anger and intolerance. Anti-Jewish attacks had been known in northern Europe before 1096, most notably after 1009, but the repeated ferocity of attacks by crusaders indicates that the wars of the cross lent spurious justification to such communal barbarism. Yet the attacks on the Jews signal a piety of sorts, however underpinned by ignorance, larceny, and criminality. To suggest mixed motives for many crusaders does not convict them of hypocrisy, merely complexity.

It has become fashionable to ascribe purely mercenary inspiration to the citizens of the Italian maritime cities, in a peculiar modern historiographical combination of retrospective snobbery and a belief that commerce is 'modern' and so immune from 'naïve' or 'medieval' religious sincerity. Material advantage and genuine religious commitment have never been mutually exclusive; nor were they among crusaders. The Venetian crusade of 1122–5, in a sort of foreshadowing of the Fourth Crusade, raided Byzantine territory to force a restoration of preferential trade rules. Yet it also fought a hard sea battle against the Egyptians and helped capture the port of Tyre, again in return for trading privileges and property. On return to the Adriatic further raiding carried off booty and relics. Modern disapproval misses the essence. The Italian trading cities' contributions to crusading of men, blood, treasure, and materials were second to none. Crusading enthusiasm did not stop at the gates of commercial ports, nor did the desire for profit or, at least, an avoidance of loss contradict the spirituality as well as the material risks inherent in taking the cross, any more than did a knight's desire to fight to earn salvation and to survive. While elements of duty, fear, devotion, repentance, excitement, adventure, material profit, and escapism feature in the sources as contributory spurs to action, one overwhelming urge, with secular and spiritual dimensions, may have been what could inadequately be described as status – with church, peers, neighbours, relatives, God. The most typical trophies of this status were relics which the returning crusader bestowed on local churches, further enhancing both social reputation and godly credit; the lure of the unique richness of treasure houses of Christian relics at Constantinople acted as a spur to its destruction in 1204. The discredit afforded those who failed to fulfil their vows, or those who deserted or refused to enlist, alone reflected the continuing social admiration that clung to veterans of the cross.

It is often argued that the crusade declined as a political, religious, and social force from the mid-13th century. This has been attributed to a growth in the wealth of western Europe, which is supposed to have begun a process of 'modernization' in which crusading appeared old hat as a cause inspired by God not Mammon. The decadence of crusading has been attributed variously to the corruption of money in the professionalization of the business of the cross and to the rise of national self-interest over the demands of Christendom in general. The diversion of holy war to internal enemies of the papacy has been taken as a barometer of this decay. Many of these arguments refer to the Holy Land crusade and make little sense applied elsewhere. It is undeniable that papal crusades in Italy aroused the anger of clerics who had to pay taxes for them or political opponents; successive popes trod carefully to avoid inciting opposition. Preaching for internal crusades tended to be far more restricted geographically than that for eastern expeditions, and there persisted a nervous sensitivity to local feeling if internal crusades were to be preached in parallel or in competition with eastern campaigns. Yet much of the hostility to the anti-Hohenstaufen or Italian crusades in the 13th and 14th centuries, beyond the overtly partisan, revolved around anxieties lest they diverted attention from the plight of the Holy Land. The business of the cross retained its popularity, even if its adherents were more discriminating than papal apologists hoped or imagined. The rise of stronger national regimes delivered a more damaging blow. By appropriating political energy, material resources, and even holy war mentalities, the Hundred Years' War between England and France (1337–1453) sealed the loss of the Holy Land as decisively as the military system of the Mamluk Empire. Fighting for God remained an ideal and practice throughout the later Middle Ages and beyond, its legal implications absorbed into secular as well as canon law codes. Libraries were full of crusade histories and romances; veterans' artefacts became cherished heirlooms; illuminated manuscripts, theatrical re-enactments, paintings, tiles, and tapestries in palaces, houses, and town halls kept the images fresh. However quixotic it may seem to blinkered modern eyes peering at the past for the origins of our own world, the Christian holy war we call the Crusades, partly because of its lack of rigid definition and protean adaptability, had seeped into the bedrock of western public consciousness through social and religious as well as political and military channels, embodying many of the human qualities and inspiring martial actions that remained highly regarded for centuries after Outremer had faded into a golden memory.

# Chapter 7
# **Holy lands**

Crusading sacralized the lands it attacked or conquered. These were seen in terms of recovery of the heritage of Christ (Palestine), His Mother (Livonia), or His disciples, such as James (Spain) and Peter (any region placed under papal protection or lordship). Less obviously, crusading also tended to sacralize the lands from which the holy warriors had been drawn. The numinous distinction bestowed by participation in crusading merged with concepts of just wars fought for the *patria*, the homeland. These consecrations provoked a series of anomalies between image and reality. Crusade frontiers, in Spain, Syria, Prussia, or Livonia, were at once ideologically rigid while physically, culturally, or politically porous. Promoters and chroniclers of conquest proclaimed sharp religious and ethnic divisions when economic contact and the mechanics of lordship required social exchange leading to cultural transmission. The universal homeland of these New Israelites, Christendom (*Christianitas*), became fragmented into distinct *patria*, kingdoms or cities, appropriating to themselves the concept of a 'Holy Land' where, for the political elite, involvement in the crusade stood as a touchstone of identity, respect, and authority. Crusading stood as an objective of national policy and an analogy for national war. No less than the holy lands of crusader conquest, these *patria* were bolstered by images derived from the Israel of the Old Testament and egregious apocalyptic political propaganda and thought, in which any successful crusader king could lay claim to the prophecies of the Last Emperor at the End of Time. The consequent habit of equating national aggression with transcendent universal good and vice versa constitutes a lasting inheritance. 'One nation under God' has a complex ancestry but it includes the medieval holy wars of the cross.

## The holy land overseas: Outremer and colonial myths

Shortly after the First Crusade, the northern French writer and abbot Guibert of Nogent coined the phrase 'Holy Christendom's new colonies' for the Christian conquests in Syria and Palestine. The question of whether the Christian settlements in the east can be described as colonies in any modern sense has exercised historians for two centuries. If a colony can be understood as, in some fashion, deliberately created to act as a subordinate in a larger commercial, economic, or strategic system operated by a distant colonial power in its own interests, then Outremer, despite its name, hardly fits the model. If, however, a colony implies a plantation of an alien population of rulers and settlers who retain their cultural identity and association with their regions of origin, then Outremer displays colonial characteristics. However, Outremer formed part of no secular or ecclesiastical western empire except as provinces of the Latin Church. Unlike Prussia, the kingdom of Jerusalem, while paying Peter's Pence to the papacy, was not a papal fief, and in the 13th century fiercely resisted attempts to incorporate it into the Hohenstaufen empire. Despite intimate dynastic links with western aristocracies, no trans-Mediterranean lordships were created. Despite a constant flow of pilgrims and, in the 12th century, settlers in both directions, contacts between immigrants and their countries of origin quickly faded, Franks tending to adopt local places as surnames. No reigning Frankish monarch of Jerusalem ever visited western Europe.

While the constant need for western reinforcement and an increasing reliance on the international networks of Italian commercial cities and of the Military Orders never permitted relations between Outremer and the west to lose their umbilical quality, the polity of Outremer (12th-century Byzantine claims to Antioch excepted) remained socially and institutionally autonomous. Westerners and easterners increasingly traded mocking insults about each other. Outremer's distinctive characteristic of a garrison society did not guard vital sea lanes, trade routes, markets, or sources of raw materials but what many regarded as a huge religious relic, 'Christ's heritage'. Direct material profit had not driven the conquest of Outremer, although this did not impede subsequent economic exploitation. The most self-evidently colonial element in Outremer were the representatives of the Italian commercial cities who established quarters in ports such as Acre and Tyre to house a transient population of merchants and sailors from their home ports. Most of these agents did not become permanent settlers in the east. While Outremer conformed to the medieval pattern of foreign settlements in replicating home societies rather than to the modern colonial model of voluntary or enforced dependency, it did not compare in emulation with the 13th-century Frankish establishment in Greece – 'new France' as one pope called it – in emulating the old country. In contrast with Spain and Prussia, where land frontiers with Latin Christendom ensured heavy potential immigration, or with Prussia, Livonia, and Estonia, where religious conversion of the conquered allowed a measure of acculturation of the natives with the intruders, there was no melting pot shared by immigrant and native in 12th-century Outremer. Instead, Outremer presented a mosaic of faith and ethnic communities, pieces of social tesserae wedged tightly together to form a single pattern.

Although cast in a holy land and founded by crusaders, Christian Outremer was not a 'crusader society'. While permanent peace with Muslim neighbours was, for both sides, conceptually impossible, during much of the period of Frankish occupation 1098 to 1291, truces and alliances flourished. Parts of the kingdom of Jerusalem in the mid-12th century were more peaceful than contemporary

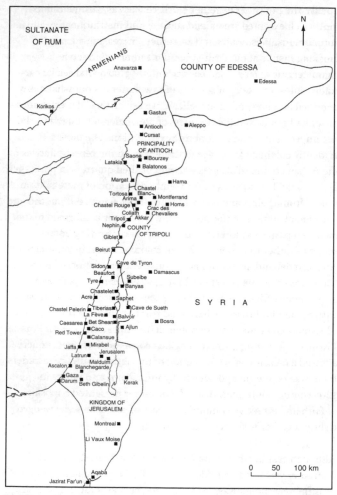

**H. The castles of Outremer**

England, France, or Italy. Most castles and fortified houses lay far from the frontiers and played the same administrative rather than military role in the organization of lordships as their counterparts did in England. The rulers and settlers were neither technically nor actually crusaders. Unlike 13th-century Prussia or Livonia, Outremer was not ruled by crusading Military Orders, however significant their role in its defence and aggression. Although the rulers' rhetoric spoke differently, with popes, politicians, and chroniclers presenting a particular frontier myth of heroic conquest and battle to justify the Franks' presence and excite western support, Outremer society, while sustained by this cohesive ideology of 'exiles' for the faith, reflected a far more humdrum diversity of experience than such crude caricatures allow.

The task of occupation fell far below the epic vision, still less did it fit either of the alternative modern interpretations of Outremer as a conduit of inter-cultural exchange and cooperation or as a bleak, arid, and doomed system of apartheid. Demographic imperatives ensured diversity in Outremer, as in its Muslim-ruled neighbours, but no deep cultural synthesis. The Franks' clothes (such as the fashionable turban or the prudent loose garments and surcoats), food, domestic architecture (even the rugged Hospitallers seem to have installed bathrooms at their castle of Belvoir), personal hygiene, and medicine were adapted to the environment. Franks learnt Arabic, a process accelerated by commerce, lordship, and the unfortunately frequent habit of their leaders getting captured and spending long years in Muslim custody. In some ways, the Frankish ruling elite resembled in status and relationship to the indigenous population the Turkish atabegs who ruled elsewhere in Syria, foreigners sustained by military strength and the extraction of revenues from an alien local labour force.

In Outremer, religion not race formed the technical test of civil rights and citizenship. Intermarriage occurred between Franks and local Christians and converted Muslims. The idea that the Franks faced an exclusively Muslim native population seems far from the

17. Crac des Chevaliers in Syria (in Arabic Hisn al-Akrad), one of the strongest and most aesthetically satisfying of the castles built by the Christian rulers of Outremer. Given to the Hospitallers in 1144, it fell to the Mamluks in 1271. In fact most Frankish forts were built away from exposed frontiers and acted as centres of administration and lordship.

case; in parts of Outremer, Muslims were not even a majority. Where necessary, Frankish rulers occasionally extended patronage to Muslim settlers, doctors, and merchants, while at the same time showing no qualms about using Muslim slave labour. A few shared sites of religious worship survived, such as in the suburbs of Acre in the 12th century, the Church of the Nativity in Bethlehem in the 13th century, or the remarkable Greek Orthodox shrine of Our Lady of Saidnaya, north of Damascus. After the initial stage of conquest, Muslim resistance to Frankish rule, in the absence of political leadership, which had fled, rarely reached beyond the level of localized banditry. The new rulers' and settlers' enjoyment of resources did not entail systematic persecution of other faith communities. Overt aggression to non-Christians seemed the preserve of zealous, boorish newcomers. In market courts at the port of Acre, jurors were drawn from both Latin and Syrian Christians and witnesses were permitted to swear oaths on their holy books – Christians on the Gospels, Jews and Samaritans on the Torah, and Muslims on the Koran – 'because', the Jerusalem law code insisted, 'be they Syrians or Greeks or Jews or Samaritans or Nestorians or Saracens, they are also men like the Franks'. The Hospitallers, who ran the great hospital in Jerusalem that could accommodate hundreds of patients at a time, agreed. They treated anyone regardless of race or religion. Only lepers were excluded, for obvious reasons.

This does not imply that Christian Outremer operated as a haven of tolerance. Medieval racism was largely cultural, revolving around external differences in customs, law, and language, more than the distinctions of blood inheritance preferred by some modern racists. In that sense, discrimination on the grounds of religion was inherently racist. This extended to the *de facto* religious discrimination against native Christian communities – Armenians, Greeks, and Arabic- or Syriac-speaking Melkites, Nestorians, Jacobites, and Maronites – not in terms of civil but ecclesiastical rights. The Franks Latinized the Church in Outremer, occupying all the top jobs and monopolizing much of the endowment and income. However, local Christians, at least in chroniclers' descriptive language, charters, and the law courts, were not confused with the Muslim settled population, the Bedouin on the borders, or the *Turci* beyond the frontiers. The Jewish population of Palestine declined sharply after 1099, although the remaining communities avoided direct persecution, many working in the dyeing business. Local Christians lived within the ambit of Frankish society and law, owning property, intermarrying, and in some rural areas actually sharing villages with immigrants, who tended to be attracted to regions already occupied by co-religionists. Muslims and Jews dwelt apart, except in towns and cities, where trade, agriculture, tax collecting, or revenue gathering brought the communities into contact. As a special distinction, all Franks were, *ipso facto*, free. Political and social barriers precluded multiculturalism just as firmly as differences of religion, race, and ethnicity. Occasionally, more general cultural hostility erupted, as in 1152 in Tripoli after the assassination of Count Raymond II, when 'all those who were found to differ either in language or dress from the Latins' were massacred. Such racial rather than religious discrimination was grounded on certain mundane but inescapable differences in language and manners: Syrians shaved their pubic hair not their beards; Franks did the reverse or neither. Yet at the non-threatening margins of civility, transmission of customs could flourish.

Although, unlike in Sicily after its 11th-century conquest by the Normans, there were few anti-Muslim riots, Outremer presented a picture of recognized diversity and enforced inequality. In 1120 laws were promulgated forbidding sexual congress between Christians and Muslims and imposing dress discrimination. The Jerusalem law code listed severe penalties for Muslim violence on Christians, but none vice versa. Taxation fell more heavily on the peasantry and most severely on Muslims, who had to pay a poll tax (as Christians had under Muslim rule). In Galilee in the 1180s, local Muslims referred to King Baldwin IV as 'the pig' and his mother, Agnes of Courtenay, as 'the sow'. One settler, encountering black Africans for the first time, 'despised them as if they were no more than seaweed'. At either end of the 12th century some Muslim communities aided invaders. In Antioch, treatment of Muslims veered from economic encouragement to extortion, prompting sporadic uprisings. Although in Muslim rural areas, and even in cities such as Tyre, public Islamic worship was permitted, Muslim shrines and cemeteries fell into disrepair and in the 1180s old men recounted tall stories of the heroic defence of the coastal cities against the invading infidel. Muslim slaves, including women in shackles, were a common sight. Without a Muslim social or intellectual elite, either in exile or denied status, their popular cultures inevitably stagnated.

Always a minority, especially in the 13th century when effectively penned in to the narrow coastal strip, the Frankish peasantry and artisans adapted to local methods of agriculture which would have been familiar, if tougher, to settlers from southern France, Italy, and Spain. Perhaps the most distinctive feature imported by westerners were pigs. The Franks lived in villages of their own, or beside local Christians, but mixed with all other groups in towns and cities. The experience of Nablus, north of Jerusalem, illustrated the tensions and accommodations of inter-communal relations. A Frankish wineshop stood opposite a Muslim guesthouse. A local Muslim woman who had married a Frank murdered him and took to a life of crime, ambushing and killing passing Franks, while the Frankish wife of a local draper became the expensive mistress of the Patriarch of Jerusalem. Not all was conflict. The Frankish viscount invited an Arab emir from northern Syria to witness a trial by battle between two Franks over allegations that one of them had set Muslim thieves onto the other's property. A bullying local Frankish landlord forced a community of devout Muslims to emigrate to Damascus while at the same time the local Samaritan sect was allowed to continue with its annual Passover ritual that attracted worshippers from across the Near East. Such practical coexistence punctuated by extremes of faith or criminality undermines neat generalizations about the colonial experience.

At the top of society, the Frankish aristocracy created a world as much like the west as possible, in law, landholding, military organization, religion, and language. However, the setting inevitably impinged. Slavery, dying out in western Christendom, formed a staple of Near Eastern society which the Franks adopted. Proximity bred contact, especially where non-Franks, even non-Christians, possessed useful talents. King Baldwin I of Jerusalem (1100–1118) took a Muslim convert as an intimate servant, probably lover, giving him his name as well as religion. The royal court of Jerusalem in the 12th century was almost as cosmopolitan as those of Norman-Graeco-Arabic Sicily or the Arab-Turkish-Kurdish-Armenian-Jewish courts of the Near East.

King Amalric (1163–74), who campaigned in Egypt and visited Constantinople, was married to a Greek, employed as family doctors and riding masters Syrian Christians who had worked for the Fatimids of Egypt and later served Saladin, and a tutor, William of Tyre (c.1130–86), steeped in the finest state of the art learning from Paris and Bologna. Some Frankish knights and nobles seemed to have forged amicable relations with Muslim counterparts across the frontiers during times of truce; a number regularly sought service with Turkish armies. Alliances between Franks and Muslim powers were commonplace, even if former allies happily slaughtered each other when the diplomatic and military wheel turned. 'Apartheid' seems an inappropriately narrow and monochrome description of such a society.

Yet Outremer did own a unique status that made integration with native non-Christians impossible. The western settlement only occurred because of the religious aspiration of the conquerors. Although the motives of immigrants remain hidden, one element in persuading non-noble settlers to try their luck in such a relatively inhospitable and distant region was the desire to live in the land where Christ and His saints had lived. The pious rhetoric of exile on one level matched the reality. With a largely immigrant higher clergy and a constant influx of lords from the west, the sense of

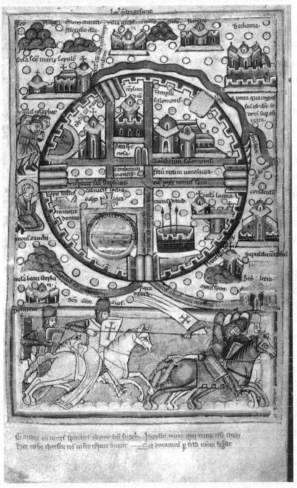

18. A formalized map of Jerusalem *c*.1170 typical of the period. The circular design reflects the image of the Holy City as the centre of the world. The Holy Sepulchre is shown in the bottom left quarter, with the Temple Mount occupying the top half. Note the crusaders fighting the Muslims in the bottom margin.

mission kept on being renewed. The holiness of the Holy Land exerted an important influence in Outremer society. The conquests of 1098–9 opened Palestine to a flood of pilgrims from Christendom with expectations fuelled by Biblical and crusading stories. At any one time, there could be 70 pilgrim ships docked at Acre, some capable of carrying hundreds of passengers. Travelling on one of the two annual 'passages', when the currents and winds in spring and autumn allowed for easier journeys, these tourists found eager hosts. The Jerusalem kings exacted tolls on them (just as their Muslim predecessors had done). The two great Military Orders of the Temple (1120) and Hospital (1113, militarized probably by 1126) were founded to protect and heal them. The catering trade grew rich on them. Residents in Outremer gave them places to visit, by sprucing up old sites, excavating others, such as the relics of the Patriarchs at Hebron in 1119, and imaginatively recreating the Biblical landscape, 'New Holy Places newly built' according to John of Würzburg in the 1160s. In re-mapping the sacred landscape, the Latin Christians were following a process familiar from the Roman emperors Titus and Hadrian in the 1st and 2nd centuries, the Greek Christians in the 4th century, the Muslims after 638, 1187, and 1291, and the Zionists and Israelis in the 20th century.

This habit of importing or annexing a new sacred landscape was common to conversion, colonization, and crusading. As on the Spanish and Baltic frontiers, in Outremer it served to reinforce a particularly strong sense of exceptionalism, at least amongst the articulate, and was of a piece with the 'fractured colonialism', as it has been described, of Frankish society. How far settlers and rulers felt the pull of divine immanence in their material surroundings can only partly be reconstructed from the opinions of their interpreters, such as William of Tyre, or from their behaviour. Those modern historians such as Joshua Prawer who have accused the Franks of cultural myopia in regard to other communities miss the point. By definition, the Frankish settlement could not overtly compromise with other ethnic models. Yet neither could – or did – they ignore them. It has become modish to condemn the western settlements in the east as a brutish intrusion into a more civilized and sophisticated Islamic world. Yet the Turkish invasion of the mid-11th century was more disruptive. The warring political and religious factions within the Islamic polity – Arab, Turkish, Kurdish, Mamluk, Sunni, Shia, Ishmaeli Assassins – created violent contest and instability only resolved by greater violence practised by unscrupulous warlords such as Zengi, Saladin, or Baibars, none of whom flinched from barbaric atrocities to further their material ends. Like the Franks, they promoted a self-serving ideology of legitimate force. Western Christians held no monopoly on intolerance, any more than they did on sanctity. Islamic lawyers warned against inter-faith fraternization; an 11th-century Baghdad legist proposed discriminatory dress for Christians and Jews. The fate of non-Christian communities in Outremer was little different to that of Christian communities under Islam. It appeared harsher because the social configuration of the remaining Muslim population, largely peasant or artisan, lacked a skilled or wealthy elite, in contrast to Muslims in Christian Spain or Christian communities in the Islamic world. This is not to deny the exclusive and discriminatory nature of Frankish rule in Outremer. However, to romanticize those whom they discriminated against is to rewrite the past to suit present sentimentality.

## The holy lands on the frontiers

*Spain*

In Spain, as in the Baltic, crusading was secondary or complementary to secular considerations and wider association of Christian conquest and holy war. A decade before the First Crusade, Alphonso VI of Castile had characterized his capture of Toledo from the Moors in 1085 'with Christ as my leader' as a restoration of Christian territory and the recreation of 'a holy place'. It is not entirely clear how far the explicit religiosity of 12th-century accounts of earlier campaigns against the Moors in Spain reflected the assimilation of crusading formulae, an older tradition of holy war or a separate local development. While defence and restoration of Christian lands matched the new rhetoric of the Jerusalem war, indigenous writers and religious leaders transformed the Iberian patronal saint, the Apostle James the Great, Santiago, into a 'knight of Christ' and heavenly intercessor for the success of Christian warfare. Such promotion of a distinctive pan-Iberian war cult helped local rulers retain ownership of their campaigns even when enjoying papal crusade privileges, while at the same time reinforcing Christian solidarity. St James, an international saint through his shrine at Compostella, did not become the exclusive preserve of any one Iberian kingdom, his cult sustaining the political ideologies of all of them. The same was generally true of the half dozen Iberian Military Orders founded in the second half of the 12th century, including one dedicated to St James.

Crusading in Spain adopted a local flavour. The great warrior kings of the 13th century, Ferdinand III of Castile (1217–52) and James I of Aragon (1213–76), rolled back the Muslim frontier self-consciously in the name of God and each flirted with carrying the fight beyond Iberia, to Africa or Palestine. Yet neither found the commitment that led their contemporary Louis IX of France to the Nile. Although some conquests, such as the capture of Cordoba by Ferdinand III in 1236, were accompanied by religious gestures of restoration and purification familiar from the eastern crusades, and in places, as at Seville (captured 1248), foreign Christian settlers were recruited, much of the Reconquista involved negotiation and accommodation of the religious and civil liberties of the conquered: James I 'the Conqueror' of Aragon's annexation of Mallorca (1229) and Valencia (1238), and Ferdinand III's conquest of Murcia (1243). Christian complaints about the calls of the muezzin persisted in some areas for centuries. Although suffering from the problems of being ruled by an elite with separate laws and religion, Muslims under Christian rule, the mudejars, and Jews and converts – *conversos* (Jewish converts to Christianity) and *Moriscos* (Muslim converts) – were a feature of Spanish life until the late 15th and 16th centuries, when a recrudescence of a manufactured neo-crusading religious militancy led to the imposition of intolerant

19. The Apostle of Christ and Holy War. A painting attributed to the Circle of Juan de Flandes (*c.*1510–20) of Saint James fighting the Moors. He is shown carrying the banner of the Spanish military order bearing his name, the Order of Santiago. The incongruity of this transformation of one of Jesus's disciples into a warrior saint escaped most medieval observers.

Christian uniformity under the Catholic monarchs Ferdinand II of Aragon (1479–1516) and Isabella of Castile (1474–1504), coinciding with the final expulsion of the Moorish rulers from Granada (1492). This new identification of a crusading mission, which persisted under Charles V and Philip II, depended as heavily on recasting Castile, in particular, as itself a new holy land with a providential world mission as it did on genuine Aragonese crusading traditions. In turn, this spawned a myth of the crusading Reconquista and the providential identity and destiny of Catholic Spain later insidiously expropriated by General Franco and his fascist apologists, academic as well as political.

The fate of Peter II of Aragon (1196–1213), father of James the Conqueror, reveals the nuances and contradictions in the Iberian experience. The 12th-century invasion of Spain by the Almohads, Muslim puritans from North Africa, had placed the Christian advances of the previous century in jeopardy. In 1212, a large international crusader host combined with Iberian kings to resist. Before confronting the Almohad forces at Las Navas de Tolosa, most of the French contingents abandoned Peter and the kings of Castile and Navarre, partly over disagreements with the local rulers' leniency towards defeated Muslim garrisons, a frontier pragmatism that, as in Palestine, struck the French as scandalous. They also did not care for the heat. The subsequent Christian victory became, as a result, almost wholly a Spanish triumph, a useful detail in the later projection of Spanish destiny. Fourteen months later Peter was defeated and killed at the battle of Muret in Languedoc by an army of French crusaders led by the church's champion, Simon de Montfort, testimony to the political cross-currents upon the surface of which crusading bobbed, and the impossibility of divorcing 'crusade' history from its secular context.

After the conquests, new (or in propaganda terms restored) sacred and secular landscapes were created, from converting mosques to churches to changing Arabic place names. In some areas, notably in Castile, immigrant settlement from further north was encouraged.

Elsewhere, the pre-conquest social and religious structures felt only modest immediate impact. It may be significant of a decline in frontier militarism that after 1300, the cult of Santiago faded before that of the Virgin Mary. Nonetheless, the holy war tradition, in its crusading wrapping, persisted amongst the knightly and noble classes, available to those engaged in wars against infidels, Muslim or heathen, a living cultural force as well as a stereotype. While his captains were observing West Africans outside the straitjacket of crusading aesthetics, the Portuguese prince Henry the Navigator (1394–1460) fervently embraced crusading aspirations and campaigned in North Africa. As late as 1578, a Portuguese king, Sebastian, at the head of an international force armed with indulgences and papal legates, fought and died in battle against the Muslims of Morocco. The penetration of Latin Christendom into the islands of the eastern Atlantic in the 14th and 15th centuries attracted crusading grants for the *dilatio*, or extension, of Christendom. The Iberian tradition ensured a sympathetic hearing for the Genoese crusade enthusiast Christopher Columbus. It formed one strand in the conceptual justification for the conquest of the Americas and, more tenuously, in the mentality of the slave trade which some saw as a vehicle for expanding Christianity. This was made possible by the idea, popular by *c.*1500, that Spain itself (however imagined) was a holy land, its Christian inhabitants new Israelites, tempered and proved in the fire of the Reconquista, championing God's cause whether against infidels outside Christendom or heretics within.

## The Baltic

On the face of it, the idea that the crusades in the Baltic were directed to conquer holy lands appears fanciful, given that the regions attacked had no Christian pre-history. Yet perhaps precisely because of its extreme incongruity, this concept gained credence: alone of the regimes established in the wake of crusader conquest, Prussia and Livonia were ecclesiastical states. The association came early. A propagandist exhortation to attack the Wends east of the Elbe in 1108 described the campaign as being to liberate 'our

Jerusalem'. This challenging analogy operated in ways that remained central to the early association of crusading with German expansion eastwards; cashing in on the new impetus to holy war provided by the Jerusalem wars; the need to defend Christendom; and the implication that the wars were aimed at recovering lost Christian land. Some lands beyond the Elbe targeted by German crusaders in the 12th century had been occupied by the Ottonian emperors before the great Slav revolt of 983 drove them back. Other areas had experienced more recent missionizing of fluctuating success. On the shifting German-Slav frontier, areas that had been conquered, even as far back as the 10th century, and then lost could attract accusations of apostasy. This confusion could work the other way; one contingent of the 1147 crusaders found themselves besieging recently Christianized Stettin.

The distinctive character of the Baltic crusades lay in the explicit alliance of crusade and conversion, or, as saintly Bernard of Clairvaux put it, conversion or extermination. Innocent III freely employed the language of compulsion to 'drag the barbarians into the net of orthodoxy'. This unsound doctrine acknowledged the religious component in ethnicity, cultural identity, and racial awareness. In contrast with Spain or the Near East, in the Baltic, conversion came as the inevitable corollary and recognition of conquest. Paradoxically, this allowed for greater cultural accommodation and transmission from Slav to German and vice versa. Descendants of the pagan Wendish prince Niklot, victim of the first crusader attack in 1147 and killed by Christians in 1160, became the Germanized princes and dukes of Mecklenberg, one of whom joined a crusade to Livonia in 1218. However repellent to the religiously fastidious, enforced conversion worked; by 1400 the Baltic had become a Latin Christian lake, even if elements of pagan culture swam freely beneath the surface. Conversion not backed by coercion would have had a harder struggle, as the successful resistance of pagan Lithuania showed, only accepting conversion undefeated on its own terms in 1386. The application of crusading incentives from the mid-12th century did not manufacture this link between force and faith, it merely recognized a process of cultural and political imperialism already well established.

Crusading in the Baltic contributed to the 12th-century German expansion into territory between the Elbe and Oder and western Pomerania; 13th-century German penetration into the southern Baltic lands between the Vistula and Niemen, Prussia, Courland, and later, in the 14th century, Pomerelia west of the Vistula; the transmarine colonization of Livonia by a combination of churchmen and merchants from German trading centres such as Lübeck and Bremen; the aggressive expansionism of the Danish crown, especially in northern Estonia; and the advance of the Swedes into Finland. Until the 13th century crusading, as opposed to more general associations of war with Divine favour, played only an intermittent role. The application of crusade privileges to the summer raids on the western Wends during the Second Crusade in 1147 had more to do with buying Saxon support and internal peace within the empire in Conrad III's absence in the Holy Land than the institution of a new sustained crusade front. One of the protagonists in the 1147 expeditions, Albert the Bear, did not need crusade privileges to carve out a principality of Brandenberg beyond the Elbe; his territorial acquisitiveness was in any case portrayed by apologists as attracting God's approval. Such conquests went together with the implanting of bishoprics and monasteries and so earned clerical plaudits. The secular reality was brutal for the conquered, harsh for the German and Flemish settlers, and, as one pious frontier priest lamented, encouraged the avarice rather than the piety of another 1147 crusader, Henry the Lion, duke of Saxony. Between 1147 and 1193 only one papal crusade grant was directed towards the Baltic, in 1171. However, the often savage wars of conquest and conversion conducted against the Slavs by the German princes and kings of Denmark were recognized by the papacy as 'inspired with the heavenly flame, strengthened by the arms of Christ, armed with the shield of faith and protected by divine favour', as Alexander III put it in 1169. Nonetheless, to ascribe responsibility for medieval German imperialism on the

crusade would be misleading; one might as well accuse the
Christian Church. It might also be added that the Baltic pagans
were no less keen on massacring opponents and eradicating
symbols of an alien faith. Although, except in Lithuania, the pagan
holy wars ended in defeat, this does not mean they did not happen.

The real impetus towards affixing technical apparatus of crusading
– vow, cross, indulgence, and so on – to Christian conquest in the
Baltic came when attention shifted from the western Slavs of the
southern Baltic to the heathen tribes further east, in Livonia,
Estonia, Finland, and Prussia, the theatres of crusading operations
that dominated the period from the 1190s. While defence of the
missionary churches established in Livonia or Estonia around 1200
were relatively easily justified, support for extensive conquests in
either region, still less in Prussia, demanded these areas acquire a
new holy status. Each answered this need in different ways. The
campaigns of the kings of Denmark along the southern Baltic coast
and the southern shore of the Gulf of Finland in northern Estonia
attracted sporadic papal grants of crusade privileges familiar
elsewhere, while the monarchs surrounded themselves with the
useful aura of Christian warriors, 'active knights of Christ', to justify
foreign conquest and internal authority. The pagans were to be
rooted out by force and Christendom expanded. Here the
conquerors were performing holy tasks and thus their conquests,
by incorporation into Christendom, became *ipso facto* holy.

Away from the muddled but powerful religiosity of Christian
monarchy, the consecration of crusade targets followed more
precise lines. From *c*.1202, the missionary bishop of Riga recruited
a religious order of knights, the Militia of Christ or Sword Brothers,
to defend and extend his diocese in Livonia centred on the River
Dvina. A few years later his colleague on the Polish-Prussian
frontier assembled a similar body, the Militia of Christ of Livonia
against the Prussians, also known as the Knights of Dobrin (or
Dobryzin) after their original headquarters on the Vistula. Again,
the status of the conquests was defined by that of the conquerors,

bishops, and sworn professed, as well as professional, knights of Christ. The dedication of the Christian settlement created at Riga by the missionaries and merchants to the Virgin Mary allowed Livonia to be depicted as the land of the Mother of God, her dowry, allowing crusade apologists in the region to describe crusaders there as pilgrims or 'the militia of pilgrims'. This brought them further into line with crusaders elsewhere; even crusaders against the Albigensians were called pilgrims by some, almost as a *sine qua non* of legitimacy. The first two churches built in the new town of Riga before 1209 were dedicated to Mary, the patroness, and Peter, the guarantor of ecclesiastical privileges. When the Teutonic Knights took over war and government in both Prussia and Livonia in the 1230s, absorbing the other military orders in the process, and from 1245 the direction of a permanent crusade in the region, the identification with the Virgin Mary was complete, as she was the patroness of the German order. In Livonia the knights bore her image as a war banner. With the papacy designating Prussia a papal fief (as part of its anti-imperial policy) in 1234, the Teutonic Knights' territory was doubly sanctified. In the absence of a historic justification for war, a late 13th-century rhyming chronicle from Livonia, probably by a Teutonic Knight, insinuated a transcendent context. Beginning his work with accounts of the Creation, Pentecost, and the missions of the Early Church, the author admitted that no apostle reached Livonia, unlike the myth of James converting Spain. Instead, a higher mission was being pursued in the wastes of the eastern Baltic, the holy task begun by the Apostles of proselytizing the world now carried forward through service and death in the armies of the Mother of God in defence of Her land.

Such literary devices could reassure participants and attract recruits while not fully reflecting the nature of war in Prussia, Livonia, and Estonia. Not all enemies were pagan. In Estonia, the Teutonic Knights competed for power with fellow crusaders, the Danes. In 1242 an attack on the Orthodox Christians of Russian Pskov ended in the famous defeat on Lake Peipus/Chud by

Alexander Nevsky, evocatively imagined in Eisenstein's memorable propagandist film. In Prussia, especially in the west, German and Flemish settlement appeared substantial; in Livonia and Estonia, only accessible by a tricky and expensive sea voyage when the water was free of ice, negligible and almost exclusively limited to the fortified religious trading posts on the main rivers. Prussia witnessed a slow process of acculturation similar to that between the Elbe and the Oder. Slavs became Germans, an uncomfortable thought for later racial nationalists on both sides of the linguistic divide. The judicial pluralism and segregation familiar from other crusading fronts did not prevent the Prussians adopting elements of German inheritance laws. Over generations, the brutality of forced conversion, occupation, alien settlement, and discrimination against natives transformed Prussia into a distinctively German province. By contrast, only a small military, clerical, and commercial elite survived in Estonia and Livonia, where the Teutonic Knights remained until 1562, 37 years after the order's secularization in Prussia. In the shadow of this past, Hitler, with his obscenely warped historical squint, rejected the loss of any part of Prussia from the Reich, demanding Memel, established by the German invaders in 1252, from the Lithuanians in March 1939, an act that provoked Britain's guarantee to protect Poland. Yet a few months later, he consigned the Baltic states to the lot of the Russians as if they were less 'German'.

However, the link from the Teutonic Knights to the SS and the nationalized racism of the Third Reich, lovingly traced by Himmler and his historically illiterate ghouls, relied on rancid imagination not fact. The crusades did not drive the expansion of German power, nor the expansion of Spain. Wider cultural, economic, demographic, social, and technological forces did that. In so far as these impulses were articulated in religious terms, crusading offered a particular vocabulary, both practical and inspirational, that could service self-referential ideologies and self-righteous policies of domination. Holy symbols achieved cultural and political significance, the Catholic churches and churchmen transmitted a distinctive western culture, yet, for all their importance, in the expansion of Latin Christendom across its frontiers, the grammar and syntax remained resolutely secular.

## The holy lands within fortress Christendom

The image of Christendom as a beleaguered fortress, with bastions or *antemurales* opposing the advance of the infidel, had a long history. In 1089, Urban II so described the projected rebuilding of Tarragona on the Spanish coast south of Barcelona. From the 14th century, the whole concept of *antemurales* gained wide currency along the frontier with the Ottomans from Poland, through Hungary to the Adriatic. As defence of these bastions clearly formed one aspect of holy war, rulers along these frontiers themselves adopted holy war rhetoric and promoted the sacralization of their individual territories, thereby engendering a strong sense of national exceptionalism.

Away from the front line, participation in crusading also became a central feature of emergent myths and rituals of corporate or national identity. Pisa, Genoa, and especially Venice proudly proclaimed their civic involvement in the eastern crusades in art, literature, and civic ceremony. In Florence, where the cross acted as a sign both for the crusade and the city's *popolo*, or populace, participation in crusading provided opportunities to reinforce civic exceptionalism; the banner borne at Damietta in 1219 became a revered relic in the Church of San Giovanni. Similar attention to their role in crusading, especially in the east, came from the cities of northern Europe, such as Cologne and London. The Danish kings adopted the cross as their symbol around 1200. The canonization of royal holy warriors and crusaders became widespread: Charlemagne, regarded as a proto-crusader (canonized in 1166); St Eric IX of Sweden (d.1160, canonized 1167), scourge of the Finnish 'enemies of the faith'; Ferdinand III of Castile (d.1252, a recognized cult figure from the 13th century, officially canonized 1671); and Louis IX of France (d.1270, canonized 1297). Some of the legends circulated after the canonization of King Ladislas of Hungary (d.1095, canonized 1192) portrayed him as the lost leader of the First Crusade, in fact evoking the career of Bela III (d.1196) who had sponsored Ladislas' sanctification. Politically and diplomatically having pulled Hungary, like Denmark and later Poland, towards Latin Christendom, the crusades were then recruited to sanctify local royal dynasticism.

This association was most evident in France. The French kings' habit of crusading helped create what has been called the 'religion of monarchy' with its elevation of the kingdom by royal propagandists from c.1300 into a Holy Land, and the French as God's Chosen People. A striking illuminated manuscript produced at Acre c.1280 depicted Louis IX at Damietta in 1249 emblazoned with fleurs de lis; there is not a cross in sight. The crusade and the providential destiny of France and its ruling dynasty merged in the later Middle Ages into a form of apocalyptic royal or national messianism. One contemporary prophesied that Joan of Arc's victories over the English in 1429 would result in her leading King Charles VII (1422–61) to conquer the Holy Land, a theme recalled in 1494 when Charles VIII of France (1483–98) launched his invasion of Italy by declaring his intention to recover Jerusalem. Even after the French religious polity had been shattered by the Reformation and the destructive Wars of Religion in the second half of the 16th century, the image of crusading as the special preserve and responsibility of 'the Most Christian Kings' of France (a 12th-century courtesy title) survived among both Catholic and Huguenot apologists of Henry IV (1589–1610). This French experience found a close parallel in late medieval Spain, in particular Castile, where a prophetic tradition nurtured by the Reconquista inspired a sense that the Iberian holy wars required ultimate fulfilment in the recovery of Jerusalem. The expulsion of the Moors from Granada led to North African forays by Ferdinand and his grandson Charles V (1516–55) which were cast by royal polemicists as preludes to the recovery of the Holy Sepulchre. For

20. Louis IX of France attacks Damietta in Egypt, June 1249, from a manuscript written and drawn at Acre in the Holy Land *c*.1280. It is notable that there is not a cross in sight; instead the crusaders are shown bearing the fleur de lis, royal emblem of France.

Charles's son, Philip II (1555–98), the synergy of God's war and Spain's war occupied the centre of his worldview.

This transformation of lands of crusaders into crusading kingdoms and thus into holy lands went one step further by harnessing the model of the Old Testament Israelites and the Maccabees defending God's heritage, which had occupied a prominent place in traditional crusade semiotics. If the Holy Land or Christendom were *patria*, why not the crusaders' own kingdoms or city states? Pope Clement V's answer in 1311 was clear: 'Just as the Israelites are known to have been granted the Lord's inheritance by the election of Heaven, to perform the hidden wishes of God, so the kingdom of France has been chosen as the Lord's special people.' Others could play the same game. Reflecting on English victories in the Hundred Years' War to parliament in 1377, Chancellor Haughton, bishop of St David's, commented that 'God would never have honoured this land in the same way as he did Israel . . . if it were not that He had chosen it as his heritage'. One popular verse of the time even suggested that 'the pope had become French, but Jesus had become English'. God's career as an Englishman had many centuries to run.

These Scriptural borrowings operated within a pre-crusading tradition of finding Old Testament precedents for the defence of homelands, and cannot necessarily be linked directly with crusading. However, the language employed by those attempting to sacralize national warfare was so congruent to current crusade rhetoric as to make neat distinctions impossible; propagandists probably deliberately elided the two. Of course, not all national holy wars were associated with crusading. The Hussites in 15th-century Bohemia self-consciously created their own holy land, renaming cult sites after places in Palestine, such as Mount Tabor or Mount Horeb, while rejecting utterly the crusade tradition that fuelled the campaigns launched against them. By contrast, within Catholic Christendom, from the 14th century crusading motifs were increasingly recruited to national causes, such as the conflicts between France and Flanders, England and Scotland, and, most pervasively, England and France. Occasionally, as in 1383 or 1386, actual crusade grants were applied to campaigns in the Hundred Years' War. More frequently, language and images of holy war made familiar by crusading were inserted into descriptions or justifications of events. Henry V's chaplain presented the English at Agincourt (1415) as 'God's people', dressed 'in the armour of penitence', encouraged by their king to follow the example of Judas Maccabeus. Such transference was eased by the ubiquitous appropriation of the cross as national uniform across Europe in the later Middle Ages (for example, the red cross of the English), a symbol that spoke more loudly than legal or canonical logic-chopping. There were many influences on the creation of national holy lands and the sacralizing of political rule and identity in the later Middle Ages. In so far as self-defining civic, dynastic, or national conflicts adopted some ideological and rhetorical features derived from the most charismatic expression of medieval holy war, the crusade was one of them.

# Conclusion
# Crusading our contemporary

Long before the last Roman Catholic took the cross, perhaps in the early 18th century for the Habsburgs against the Ottomans in central Europe or the kings of Spain against Muslim pirates in the Mediterranean, the history and legends of the Crusades had entered the mythic memory of Christian Europe.

From the First Crusade, the wars of the cross had been sustained, developed, and refined by concurrent description and interpretation, popular and academic. By the 15th century, appreciation of what passed for crusade history underpinned all serious discussion of future projects. Provoked by immediate political concerns, such studies tended to polemic and self-interest, blind to the distinction between legend and evidence. From humanist scholarship and theological hostility in the 16th century emerged a more independent historiography. The academic study of crusading – or holy war as it was generally called – was encouraged and distorted by the two great crises that threatened to tear Christendom apart: the advance of the Ottomans and the Protestant reformations.

The 16th and early 17th centuries secured the continued cultural prominence of the Crusades. Much of the responsibility for this lay with Protestant scholars in Germany and France. Despite Roman Catholics seeking crusading privileges when fighting Protestants, admiration for the faith and heroism of the crusaders crossed confessional divides, as did fear of the Ottoman Turks. The refusal of certain Protestant scholars to dismiss crusading simply as a papal corruption provided a bridge between the Roman Catholic past and what they imagined as the Protestant future. The Crusades were rendered as national achievements, ecumenical even, at a time when religious passions still burned violently. Elevating the Crusades away from partisan religious ownership allowed the past to be reconciled with the present through inherited national identities, a process that contributed to the creation of a secular concept of Europe.

As long as the Catholic Church attached crusading apparatus to wars against the Turks and confessional enemies, and political and social radicalism were articulated in religious terms, some still found it controversial. For others, crusading slipped into the quiet reaches of history, settling into channels of moral and religious disapproval or admiration for distant heroism, often tinged with nationalism. With the evaporation of the Ottoman threat in the 18th century, past wars against Islam could be viewed with detached rather than engaged prejudice. Observers of the apparently defeated culture could indulge their tastes for the exotic and the alien with the frisson of danger replaced by a thrill of superiority lent intellectual respectability by emerging concepts of change and progress. Fear of the Turks gave way to contempt, fascination, and a sort of cultural and historical tourism. Muslims in the Near East, increasingly accessible as the sea-lanes became passable, were transformed from demons to curiosities. Such concerns produced an inevitable narrowing of focus onto crusades to the Holy Land and Christian Outremer. They also made the emotions behind crusading seem even more remote.

The prevalent 18th-century intellectual attitude, lit by anti-clericalism, was set in a disdainful grimace at what was caricatured as the ignorance, fanaticism, and violence of earlier times. Yet Gibbon's 'World's Debate' appeared to have been won by the west, with European successes in Mogul India supplying further consolation and confirmation of superiority. External stimulus to shifting perceptions came from the elite fashion for Oriental and Near Eastern artefacts and the direct contact with the Levant following Napoleon Bonaparte's campaign in Egypt and Syria in 1798–9 and the opening up of the region to upper-class tourists, from Châteaubriand to Benjamin Disraeli, whose romantic instincts were stirred by what they saw or imagined. The past required re-arrangement to suit these new enthusiasms and assumptions. Thus discussion of the Crusades to the east had to dwell more on the motives and behaviour of the crusaders rather than the dismal outcome of their exertions, on cultural values and potential rather than undoubted failure. The Crusades were refashioned into a symbol of western valour and cultural endeavour, a process encouraged by the growing popularity of another form of 'otherness' to contrast with the self-perceived modernity of Enlightenment Europe – medievalism. The early 19th century saw the combination of Orientalism and medievalism revive crusading as a set of literary references. As an example of passion over pragmatism, the Crusade became an analogy for romantic or escapist policies of those troubled by creeping capitalism and industrialization. The political exploitation of the history of the Crusades possessed a sharper edge in continental Europe, where it became a tool of reaction against the ideals and practices both of the French Revolution and liberalism. The new cult of neo-chivalry supplied moral, religious, and cultural as well as actual architectural buttresses for an aristocratic *ancien régime* losing much of its exclusivity if not power.

From the late 18th century, the word 'crusade' was applied metaphorically or analogously to any vigorous good cause. More precisely, in the absence of devastating general conflicts after 1815, 19th-century Europe spawned a cult of war which could be projected back onto the Crusades. The association of just causes and sanctified violence, sealed with the confused sentimentality of Romantic neo-chivalry, found stark concrete form in war

memorials across western Europe after the First World War, a
conflict regularly described by clergy as well as by politicians as 'a
great crusade'; bishops might have been expected to know better.
More scrupulous observers cavilled at such meretricious rhetoric,
yet the imagery persisted even when the idealism had drowned in
Flanders mud; General Eisenhower's Order for the Day of 6 June
1944 described the D-Day offensive as 'a great crusade'. The
connection with spiritually redemptive holy warfare had become
drained of much meaning. Any conflict promoted as transcending
territorial or other material aims could attract the crusade epithet,
increasingly a lazy synonym for ideological conflict or, worse, a
sloppy but highly charged metaphor for political conflicts between
protagonists from contrasting cultures and faiths. In ways
unimaginable when Runciman denounced the morality of
crusading in the mid-20th century, the Crusades no longer just
haunt the memory but stalk the streets of 21st-century
international politics, in particular in the Near East. In an irony
often lost on protagonists, these public perceptions of the Crusades
that underpin confrontational rhetoric derive from a common
source. The Near Eastern radical or terrorist who rails against
'western' neo-crusaders is operating in exactly the same conceptual
and academic tradition as those in the west who continue to
insinuate the language of the crusade into their approach to the
problems of the region. This is by no means a universal set of
mentalities, as demonstrated from the literary and academic cliché
of a civilized medieval Islamic world brutalized by western
barbarians, to the almost studiously anti-crusading rhetoric and
policies of NATO and others in the Balkan wars of the 1990s, to
opposition to the crude caricaturing of Islam after September 2001.
The re-entry of the Crusades into the politics of the Near East is
baleful and intellectually bogus.

President Bush II and Usama bin Laden are co-heirs to the legacy of
a 19th-century European construct. Here, one of the most
influential historians of the Crusades was Joseph François Michaud
(1767–1839). A publishing entrepreneur, Michaud combined

uncritical antiquarianism with a keen sense of the market and prevailing popular sentiment. A monarchist, nationalist, and anti-Revolutionary Christian, Michaud allied admiration for the Crusades' ideals with a supremacist triumphalism over Islam. He helped provide apparent historical legitimacy for colonialism and cultural imperialism, increasingly the litmus test of European hegemony and national status. Thus crusading could be transmuted into a precursor of Christian European superiority and ascendancy, taking its place in what was proclaimed as the march of western progress. Michaud's convenient and seductive vision left an indelible stain.

Yet Arab, Arabist, and Islamic outrage ignored the uncomfortable fact that Michaud's construct played its part in setting their own agenda too. In rallying opinion against European intrusion, the Ottoman Sultan Abdulhamid II (1876–1909) labelled their imperialism as a crusade, his remark that 'Europe is now carrying out a Crusade against us in the form of a political campaign'. Much subsequent Islamic discourse on western attitudes to the Crusades and the Near East has been coloured by a negative acceptance of the Michaud version of history as if this were the immutable western response or historically accurate. No continuity exists in Arabic responses to western aggression between medieval crusading and modern political hostility, any more than there is between medieval and modern *jihad*, except in rhetoric and an ahistorical appeal to the past. Assumptions of an inherent conflict of power and victimization that elevates a wholly unhistorical link between modern colonialism and medieval crusading. It is Michaud in a mirror. Occidentalism and Orientalism share the same western frame. The idea that the modern political conflicts in the Near East or elsewhere derive from the legacy of the Crusades or are being conducted as neo-crusades in anything except extremist diatribe is deceitful.

All sides seem reluctant to accept that the images of crusade and *jihad* introduced into late 20th- and 21st-century conflicts are not

**COOK'S CRUSADER.**

*Imperial Knight-Templar (the German Emperor—to SALADIN).* "WHAT!! THE CHRISTIAN POWERS PUTTING PRESSURE UPON YOU, MY DEAR FRIEND!! HORRIBLE! I CAN'T THINK HOW PEOPLE CAN DO SUCH THINGS!"

21. *Punch* lampoons Kaiser Wilhelm II of Germany's vainglorious trip to the Holy Land in 1898 by referring to the travel company that booked his package tour. In fact, at the time the Germans were more interested in recruiting Turkish and Muslim support against Britain and France.

time-venerated traditions of action or abuse, but modern imports. It has been observed that no Islamic state has formally launched a *jihad* against a non-Muslim opponent since the demise of the Ottoman Empire after the First World War. Even that Islamic holy war had been sponsored and encouraged by the Turks' German allies. Most African and Near Eastern *jihads* proclaimed in the 19th century and since were not against infidel imperialists but Islamic rivals, oppressors, and heretics or for religious reform. This is not to deny the presence of *jihad* language and theory, as in the propaganda of states at war with the State of Israel in 1948, 1967, or 1973. However, there is nothing old-fashioned, still less 'medieval', about the techniques, recruitment, or ideology of al-Qaeda. The devious polemical association between 'crusaders' and 'Jews' is historical nonsense. Al-Qaeda's international reach is a creation of modernity and globalization as surely as the World Wide Web. Many states most disliked by those who claim to be fearful of Islam are explicitly secular. Yet fanciful analogies with crusading have accompanied most major conflicts in the eastern Mediterranean from the First World War onwards, including unlikely associations such as the siege of Beirut in 1982 with the siege of Acre in 1189–91. The Arabic propaganda transmuting Israelis into crusaders is a direct consequence of this. Whilst on their side some Israeli extremists hark back to an older tradition of almost Maccabean revivalism, others are content to re-fashion their landscape to exclude, in place names or archaeological designation, Arabic traces, seeing the State of Israel as a liberation not an occupation. There are obvious historic parallels with Christian Outremer, but also with Umayyad Palestine or Roman Syria – conquerors imposing their own space. However, Israelis are not the new crusaders, any more than the Americans. Saddam Hussein was not the new Saladin, even though they shared a birthplace.

To imagine otherwise goes beyond fraudulence. It plays on a cheap historicism that at once inflames, debases, and confuses current conflicts, draining them of rational meaning or legitimate solution.

22. A propaganda poster showing Saladin and President Saddam Hussein of Iraq. Both were born in Tikrit, northern Iraq. Ironically, Saladin was a Kurd, people Saddam Hussein persecuted and massacred.

The Crusades reflected central human concerns of belief and identity that can only be understood on their own terms, in their own time; so, too, their adoption and adaptation by later generations. While it is tempting to draw conclusions derived from geographical congruity or superficial political similarities, the land in which Jakelin de Mailly fell over 800 years ago and the cause for which he died held truths for his time, not ours.

# Further reading

Historically, the study of the Crusades has usually been marked by prejudice, bias, and judgementalism. Very little surviving primary evidence is without inherent distortion. Later interpretations have consistently reflected the concerns of the historians rather than objective assessment of the phenomenon. Medieval observers represented the Crusades in a scriptural context as signifiers of divine providence. Since the 16th century, shifting religious, political, and intellectual fashions have determined very different presentations: confessional or philosophical disdain, romantic exoticism, assumptions of cultural conflict, colonial apologetics, imperialism, and nationalism. Some have always sought to frame the Crusades as a mirror of the modern age, reassuring or troubling in similarities or contrasts. Modern scholarship, while embracing a far wider range of sources, from canon law to archaeology, is no less prone to factionalism, the influence of politics, as in the Israeli school led by Joshua Prawer, or of conflicting metaphysical constructs of the past. On the contentious issue of definition, the ecclesiastical historian Giles Constable has characterized the competing interpreters as **generalists**, who locate the origins and nature of crusading in the long development of Christian holy war before 1095; **popularists**, who favour the idea that crusading emerged as an expression of popular piety; **traditionalists** who insist on the centrality of Jerusalem and the Holy Land to legitimate crusading; and **pluralists**, who concentrate on pious motivation, canon law, and papal authorization to include all conflicts enjoying the privileges of wars of the cross regardless of destination or purpose. Such academic disputes may appear arcane. Yet they matter if understanding of the past is to be liberated from oversimplified and misleading public history and the maw of modern polemic. Having previously wreaked so much havoc, the Crusades should not be recruited to the battlegrounds of the 21st century nor yet condescendingly condemned as one of Christianity's legion of aberrations.

## General

M. Barber, *The New Knighthood* (Cambridge, 1994)

C. Erdmann, *The Origins of the Idea of Crusading*, tr. Marshall W. Baldwin and Walter Goffart (Princeton, 1977) (the classic **generalist** text)

A. Forey, *The Military Orders* (London, 1992)

C. Hillenbrand, *The Crusades: Islamic Perspectives* (Edinburgh, 1999)

N. Housley, *The Later Crusades* (Oxford, 1992) (**pluralist**)

H. E. Mayer, *The Crusades*, 2nd edn. (Oxford, 1988) (**traditionalist**)

J. Riley-Smith, *The Crusades: A Short History* (London, 1987) (**pluralist**)

J. Riley-Smith (ed.), *The Oxford Illustrated History of the Crusades* (Oxford, 1995)

J. Riley-Smith, *What Were the Crusades?*, 3rd edn. (London, 2002) (**pluralist**)

S. Runciman, *A History of the Crusades* (Cambridge, 1951–4) (**traditionalist**, once described as 'the last great medieval chronicle')

C. Tyerman, *The Invention of the Crusades* (London, 1998)

## Holy war

N. Housley, *Religious Warfare in Europe 1400–1536* (Oxford, 2002)

J. Muldoon, *Popes, Lawyers and Infidels* (Liverpool, 1979)

F. H. Russell, *The Just War in the Middle Ages* (Cambridge, 1975)

## Holy lands

R. Barlett, *The Making of Europe* (London, 1993)

E. Christiansen, *The Northern Crusades*, 2nd edn. (London, 1997)

D. Lomax, *The Reconquest of Spain* (London, 1978)

J. Prawer, *The Latin Kingdom of Jerusalem* (London, 1972)

R. C. Smail, *Crusading Warfare* (Cambridge, 1956)

### The business of the cross

J. Brundage, *Canon Law and the Crusader* (Madison, 1969)

P. Cole, *The Preaching of the Cross to the Holy Land 1095–1270* (Cambridge, Mass., 1991)

S. Lloyd, *English Society and the Crusade 1216–1307* (Oxford, 1988)

C. Tyerman, *England and the Crusades 1095–1588* (Chicago, 1988)

### Introduction and conclusion

M. Benvenisti, *Sacred Landscape: The Buried History of the Holy Land since 1948* (London, 2000)

P. Partner, *God of Battles: Holy Wars of Christianity and Islam* (London, 1997)

E. Said, *Orientalism* (London, 1979)

E. Siberry, *The New Crusaders* (Aldershot, 2000)

# Chronology

| | |
|---|---|
| c.400 | Augustine of Hippo outlines a Christian theory of just war |
| 638 | Jerusalem is captured by the Arabs under Caliph Umar |
| 800 | Charlemagne the Frank is crowned Roman Emperor of the West |
| 9th century | Holy wars proclaimed against Muslim invaders of Italy |
| 11th century | Peace and Truce of God movements in parts of France mobilize arms bearers to protect the Church |
| 1053 | Leo IX offers remission of sins to his troops fighting the Normans of southern Italy |
| 1050s–70s | Seljuk Turks invade Near East |
| 1071 | Seljuk Turks defeat Byzantines at Manzikert; they overrun Asia Minor and establish a capital at Nicaea |
| 1074 | Pope Gregory VII proposes a campaign from the west to help Byzantium and liberate the Holy Sepulchre |
| 1095 | Byzantine appeal to Pope Urban II for military aid against the Turks; Urban II's preaching tour of France (ends 1096); Council of Clermont proclaims Crusade |
| 1096–9 | First Crusade |
| 1101 onwards | Smaller crusades to Holy Land |
| 1104 | Acre captured |
| 1107–8 | Crusade of Bohemund of Taranto against Byzantium |
| 1109 | Tripoli captured |

| c.1113 | Order of the Hospital of St John in Jerusalem recognized; militarized by c.1130 |
| 1114 onwards | Crusades in Spain |
| 1120 | Order of the Temple founded in Jerusalem to protect pilgrims |
| 1123 | First Lateran Council extends Jerusalem privileges to Spanish Crusades |
| 1144 | Edessa captured by Zengi of Aleppo |
| 1145–9 | Second Crusade |
| 1149 onwards | Further crusades in Spain and the Baltic; a few to the Holy Land |
| 1154 | Nur al-Din of Aleppo captures Damascus |
| 1163–9 | Franks of Jerusalem contest control of Egypt |
| 1169 | Saladin succeeds as ruler of Egypt |
| 1174 | Death of Nur al-Din; Saladin begins to unify Syria with Egypt |
| 1187 | Battle of Hattin; Saladin destroys army of Kingdom of Jerusalem; Jerusalem falls to Saladin |
| 1188–92 | Third Crusade |
| 1193 | Saladin dies |
| 1193–1230 | Crusades to Livonia in the Baltic |
| 1198 | Foundation of Teutonic Knights in Acre; Pope Innocent III proclaims Fourth Crusade |
| 1199 | Church taxation instituted for the Crusade; Crusade against Markward of Anweiler in Sicily |
| 1201–4 | Fourth Crusade |
| 13th century | Crusades in the Baltic by Teutonic Knights (Prussia), Sword Brothers (Livonia), Danes (Prussia, Livonia, Estonia), and Swedes (Estonia and Finland); Crusades against German peasants and Bosnians |
| 1208–29 | Albigensian Crusade |
| 1212 | Children's Crusade; Almohads defeated by Spanish Christian coalition at Las Navas de Tolosa |

| | |
|---|---|
| 1213 | Innocent III proclaims Fifth Crusade and extends crusade privileges to those who contribute but do not go on crusade |
| 1215 | Fourth Lateran Council authorizes regular crusade taxation |
| 1217–29 | Fifth Crusade |
| 1231 onwards | Crusades against the Byzantines to defend western conquests in Greece |
| 1239–68 | Crusades against Hohenstaufen rulers of Germany and Sicily |
| 1239–41 | Crusades to Holy Land of Theobald, Count of Champagne, and Richard, Earl of Cornwall; crusaders defeated at Gaza (1239) |
| 1242 | Teutonic Knights defeated by Alexander Nevsky at Lake Chud |
| 1244 | Jerusalem lost to Muslims; Louis IX of France takes the cross |
| 1248–54 | First Crusade of Louis IX of France |
| 1250 | Mamluks take rule in Egypt (to 1517) |
| 1251 | First Shepherds' Crusade |
| 1260 | Mamluks repulse Mongols at Ain Jalut; Baibars becomes sultan of Egypt (to 1277) |
| 1261 | Greeks recover Constantinople |
| 1267 | Louis IX takes cross again |
| 1268 | Fall of Antioch to Baibars of Egypt |
| 1269 | Aragonese Crusade to Holy Land |
| 1270 | Louis IX's Crusade ends at Tunis, where he dies |
| 1271–2 | Crusade to Holy Land of Lord Edward, later Edward I of England |
| 1272–91 | Small expeditions to Holy Land |
| 1282–1302 | Wars of the Sicilian Vespers; include French crusade to Aragon (1285) |
| 1289 | Fall of Tripoli |

| 1291 | Fall of Acre to al-Ashraf Khalil of Egypt and evacuation of mainland Outremer |
| 1306–1522 | Hospitallers rule island of Rhodes |
| 1307–14 | Trial and suppression of Templars |
| 14th century | Papal crusades in Italy; crusading continues against heretics in Italy; Moors in Spain; pagans in the Baltic (to 1410) |
| 1309 | Popular Crusade; Teutonic Knights move headquarters from Venice to Prussia |
| 1320 | Second Shepherds' Crusade |
| 1330s onwards | Naval leagues against Turks in Aegean |
| 1350s onwards | Ottoman Turks established in Balkans; soon establish overlordship over Byzantine emperors |
| 1365–6 | Crusade of Peter of Cyprus; Alexandria sacked (1365) |
| 1366 | Crusade of Count Amadeus of Savoy to Dardanelles |
| 1383 | Crusade of Bishop Despenser of Norwich against supporters of Pope Clement VII in Flanders |
| 1390 | Christian expedition to Mahdia in Tunisia |
| 1396 | Christian expedition against the Ottomans defeated at Nicopolis on the Danube (September) |
| 15th century | Numerous small crusading forays against the Ottomans in eastern Mediterranean and east/central Europe |
| 1420–71 | Crusades against the Hussite heretics in Bohemia |
| 1444 | Crusaders defeated at Varna in Bulgaria (November) |
| 1453 | Fall of Constantinople to Ottoman Turks under Mehmed II |
| 1456 | Belgrade successfully defended from Ottoman Turks with help of crusaders under John of Capistrano |
| 1460–4 | Abortive crusade of Pope Pius II |
| 1480 | Turks besiege Rhodes |
| 1492 | Granada falls to Spanish monarchs |

| 16th century | More crusades against Turks in Mediterranean and central Europe; from 1530s crusades threatened against heretics (Protestants) |
| --- | --- |
| 1522 | Rhodes falls to Turks |
| 1525 | Secularization of Teutonic Order in Prussia |
| 1529 | Turks besiege Vienna |
| 1530–1798 | Hospitallers rule Malta |
| 1560s–90s | French Wars of Religion; some Catholics receive crusade privileges |
| 1561–2 | Secularization of Teutonic Order in Livonia |
| 1565 | Turks fail to conquer Malta |
| 1571 | Holy League wins a naval battle against the Turks at Lepanto; Cyprus falls to Turks |
| 1578 | King Sebastian of Portugal defeated and killed at Alcazar on crusade in Morocco |
| 1588 | Spanish Armada attracts crusade privileges for Spanish |
| 1669 | Crete falls to Turks |
| 1683 | Turks besiege Vienna |
| 1684–97 | Holy League begins to reconquer Balkans from Turks |
| 1798 | Hospitallers surrender Malta to Napoleon Bonaparte |
| 1898 | Kaiser Wilhelm II of Germany visits Jerusalem and Damascus |
| 1914–18 | First World War; Ottoman Turkey allies with Germany which encourages proclamation of *jihad* against the Turks' enemies |
| 1917 | British under General Allenby take Jerusalem |
| 1919 | Versailles Peace Treaty negotiations confirm mandates for Britain and France in Syria, Palestine, Iraq, and the Lebanon |
| 1948 | Creation of the State of Israel (defended in wars 1948, 1967, 1973) |
| 1982 | Israeli invasion of Lebanon |

| 1990 | Gulf War |
| 2001 | Al-Qaeda attack on United States |
| 2003–4 | Iraq War |

# Index

## A

Abbasid dynasty 58
Abdulhamid II, Sultan 140
Absalom, Archibishop of Lund 81
Acre, Palestine 1, 115
  Fifth Crusade 39
  loss of (1291) 51
  pilgrim ships 120
  Teutonic Knights founded in 47
  Third Crusade siege of 30, 32, 142
Adalia, port of 29
Adhemar, bishop of Le Puy 22, 89, 91
Advent 90
Aelfric of Cerne, abbot of Eynsham 73
Agincourt, battle of (1415) 135
Agnes of Courtenay 116
agriculture 117
Aigues Mortes, France 7
Ain Jalut, battle of (1260) 61
al-Ashraf Khalil, sultan of Egypt 41, 62
al-Qaeda 142
Albert the Bear 127
Albigensian Crusade (1209–29) 18, 43–4, 89, 124
Aleppo, Syria 27, 30, 61
Alexander III 127
Alexandria, sack of (1365) 51
Alexius Angelus 37

Alexius I Comnenus, Emperor 21, 23, 79
Alexius III, Emperor 37
Alexius IV, co-emperor 37
Alexius V Ducan Murzuphlus, Emperor 37
Alfonso Henriques, king of Portugal 29
Alfred, king of Wessex 72
Almohads 45, 124
Alphonso VI of Castile 58, 121
Amalric, king of Jerusalem 30, 118
Ambrose of Milan 66, 69
Americas 125
Anatolia 32, 55, 58, 59, 80
Andrew, king of Hungary 39
Anna Comnena (daughter of Alexius I) 79
anti-Semitism 9, 32, 51, 85, 105–6
Antioch, Syria 23, 26, 30, 61
  battle of (1097–8) 23
  fall of (1268) 41
  Peasant's Crusade 93
  periodic uprisings 117
  principality of 26
Apocalypse 68
Aquinas, Thomas 69
Aquitaine, duchy of 21, 75
Aragon 47, 122, 124
aristocracy 19, 74, 96–7, 103, 118
Aristotle 68
Armenia 23
Arnald-Amaury, abbot of Citeaux 44
Arsuf, battle of (1191) 34
Ascalon, battle of (1099) 26

Asia Minor 29
Assad, Hafez al-, President of
    Syria 3
assassination 116
*Audita Tremendi* 94
Augustine of Hippo 66, 69–70,
    73, 82
Avars 72
Avignon, France 45
Ayyubids 80

## B

Bacon, Francis 52
Baghdad, sack of (1258) 61
Baghdad Caliphate 58, 59, 61
Baibars, sultan of Egypt 40, 41,
    62
Baldwin, Archbishop of
    Canterbury 88, 90, 91
Baldwin, Count of Flanders 36,
    38
Baldwin I, king of Jerusalem
    118
Baldwin III, king of Jerusalem
    29
Baldwin IV, king of Jerusalem
    30, 116
Baldwin of Boulogne 23
Baldwin V, king of Jerusalem
    30
Balearic Islands 47
Balkan Wars (1990s) 139
Balkans 51, 62
Baltic Crusades 18, 29, 47–50,
    53, 125–31
Baltic states 56, 57, 83, 101
Bayeux Tapestry 8
Beatitudes 66

Beirut, siege of (1982) 142
Bela III 132
Belgrade 52
Bernard, bishop of Clairvaux
    29, 50, 65, 87, 88, 89–90,
    126
Bethlehem 115
Béziers, sack of (1209) 44
Bible, The 56, 64–8, 69, 71, 76,
    109, 120, 134
Bin Laden, Usama 7, 139
bishops 74
Bohemia 44, 85, 134
Bohumund of Taranto 23
Bonet, Honoré, *Tree of Battles*
    82
Boniface of Montferrat 36
booty 106
Bosham, Hampshire 8
Bosnians 44
Bosphorus crossing (1096) 22
Bulgaria 79
Burgundy, duchy of 75
Bush, President George W. 139
Byzantine Empire 37, 58, 62,
    70, 78–9, 94
Byzantium 21, 22, 23, 56, *see
    also* Constantinople

## C

Caesarea 41
canonization 131–2
Carolingian Empire 58, 72, 73
cash redemption 99, 100, 102,
    103
Castile 45, 58, 121, 124, 132
castles, Outremer 112, 113, 114
casualty rates 103

Catalonia 58
catering trade 120
Cathars 18, 43–4, 89
Champagne, Count of 40
charitable donations 99
Charlemagne, king of the
      Franks 71–2, 131
Charles of Anjou, king of Sicily
      and Naples 45
Charles V, king of Spain 124,
      132
Charles VII, king of France 132
Charles VIII, king of France
      132
Châteaubriand, François-René
      de 138
Children's Crusade (1212) 18,
      42–3, 102
chivalric training 26
Christendom 63, 70, 72, 131–5
Christianity:
      eastern 78–9
      importance of Jerusalem
        to 14
      justification for warfare
        64–70
      militarization of western
        70–3
      shared religious sites 115
      western 64–78
Christianization 47–50, 53,
      70–1, 126–8
Christmas 90, 92
Church Fathers 66
Church of the Holy Sepulchre,
      Jerusalem 8, 15, 35, 77, 78
Cicero 69
Cistercians 89
classicism 68–9

Clement V, Pope 134
Clermont, Council of (1095)
      12–14, 21, 22, 75, 89
Clifford's Tower, York 8, 32
Clovis the Frank 71
Cluny Abbey 13
Cologne 131
colonialism 10, 110–11, 140
Columbus, Christopher 125
communes 93–4
Conrad III, king of Germany
      29, 92, 127
Constantine, Emperor 71
Constantinople 18, 94
      capture by Ottoman Turks
        52
      Christian relics 106
      Fourth Crusade 37–8, 94
      Second Crusade 29, see also
        Byzantium
contracts 99–100
Cordova:
      capture of (1236) 47, 122
      collapse of caliphate of
        (1031) 58
Cornwall, Earl of 40
Crac des Chevaliers, Syria
      114
Crete 52, 55
Cromwell, Oliver 68
cross 64, 81, 83
      taking the 88–92, 102, 105,
        see also indulgences;
        privileges
crucesignati 9, 12, 44, 88, 90,
      104
Crucifixion 14, 50
'crusade', derivation of 3
crusade sermons 86–92

Curia 81
Cyprus 32, 34, 51, 52

# D

D-Day landings (1944) 139
Dalmatia 37
Damascus, Syria 3, 6, 29–30,
    61
Damietta, Egypt:
    captured by Ayyubids 61
    captured by Louis IX 41, 131,
        132, 133
    Fifth Crusade 39, 94, 96
Danes 72, 83
Dante Alighieri 45
debt moratorium 16, 37
Denmark 21, 47, 56, 81, 127,
    128, 131, 132
diplomacy 34, 92, 98, 102
Disraeli, Benjamin 138
Doryleaum, Syria 23, 29
*Dream of the Rood* 71

# E

Easter 90, 92
ecclesiastical taxation 38, 98–9
Edessa, Armenia 23, 26, 27
Edward I, king of England 40,
    98
Egypt 18, 34, 36, 38
    Ayyubids 53, 61
    crusades impact on 57
    destruction of Levantine
        ports 41, 56, 62
    Fatimids 59, 118
    Fifth Crusade 39
    Fourth Crusade 36, 106

Louis IX's invasion of 18,
    40–1, 43
Mamluks 40, 51, 53, 60, 61–3
Napoleonic war 138
and Syria 30, *see also*
    Damietta
Egyptians 23, 26
Eisenhower, General Dwight
    D. 139
Eisenstein, Sergei 130
Elizabeth I, queen of England
    44
Emeric, king of Hungary 37
emigration 96–7
England 21, 29, 44, 45, 134,
    135
    anti-Semitism 8, 32, 50
    Norman invasion 73, 75
    taxation 98
    Third Crusade 30–4
    Viking raids on 72
English army 83
Enrico Dandolo, doge of
    Venice 37
Erdmann, Carl 71
Eric IX, king of Sweden 131
Estonia 47, 111, 128, 130
ethnic cleansing 47
Eugenius III, Pope 27
evangelism 71, 88, 92
exceptionalism 120, 131
excommunication 21
exegesis 64–8
Exodus, Book of 67

# F

fascism 124, 130
Fatimids of Egypt 59, 118

Ferdinand II of Aragon 124
Ferdinand III, king of Castile 47, 122, 131
Ferdinand V, king of Castile 132
feudalism 93, 98
Fifth Crusade (1213–29) 18, 38–40, 57, 89, 94, 96, 99
finance 93–101, 94–5
Finland 47, 53, 127, 128
First Crusade (1095–9) 16, 19–26, 58, 59, 136
    Clermont decree 12–14
    finance for 94
    lost leader of 132
    and modern imperialism 56
    and pilgrimage 77–8
    recruitment for 93
    success of 81
First Lateran Council (1123) 45
First World War (1914–18) 139, 142
Flanders 21, 22, 29, 36, 134
Florence 131
Fourth Crusade (1198–1204) 18, 36–8, 62, 106
    Cistercians 89
    funding for 94, 96
    impact of 54, 57
    recruitment 93
Fourth Lateran Council (1215) 38, 98
France 22, 134–5
    Albigensian Crusade 18, 43–4, 89, 124
    crusade of Louis IX 40–1
    ejection of Muslim pirates from 58
    expulsion of Jews 51

Fourth Crusade 36
Huguenots 44
invasion of Aragon 47
popular uprisings 42, 43
religion of monarchy 132
Second Crusade 29
taxation 98
Third Crusade 30–4
Urban II's recruitment drive in 21
Francia 74
Franco, General 124
Franks 21, 61, 117, 118, *see also* Outremer; recruitment
Frederick I, king of Germany 32, 33, 92, 100
Frederick II, king of Germany 18, 39, 45
French Revolution 138
Frisia 29
Fulk of Neuilly 88
Fulk V of Anjou 26
fundamentalism 7

G

Galilee 1, 31, 116
Genoa 52, 88, 96, 125, 131
Gerald of Wales 91
Germany 21, 22, 58, 98, 141
    Baltic crusades 47
    Baltic expansionism 126–30
    Christianized military elite 70–1
    crusaders 29
    Fifth Crusade 38
    Teutonic Knights 8, 47, 49–50, 101, 129
    Third Crusade 30–1, 47

Third Reich 130
Thirty Years War 45
Gibbon, Edward 5, 137
Gilbert of Hastings 83
Granada 47, 124, 132
Gratian of Bologna 81
Great Papal Schism 45
Greek Empire 37, 38, 52, 53–4,
     55, 56, 58, 62, 79, 111
Gregory I, Pope 66
Gregory IX, Pope 39, 99
Gregory VII, Pope 21, 76, 77
Guibert, abbot of Nogent 110
Guy, king of Jerusalem 30

H

Harold II (Godwineson), king
     of England 8
Hastings, battle of (1066) 73
Hattin, battle of (1187) 6, 30,
     31, 98
Haughton, Chancellor, bishop
     of St David's 134
Hebrew texts 13
Henry, Cardinal of Albano 90
Henry II, king of England 32,
     91, 98
Henry III, king of England 44,
     83, 102
Henry IV, Emperor of
     Germany 75–6
Henry IV, king of France 132
Henry the Lion, duke of
     Saxony 127
Henry the Navigator 125
Henry V, king of England 135
Henry VIII, king of England
     44

heresy 43–5, 56, 69, 74, 101
Hermann von Salza 49
Higden, Ranulph,
     Polychronicon 54
Himmler, Heinrich 130
Hitler, Adolf 130
Hohenstaufen dynasty 45, see
     also Frederick I; Frederick
     II
Hollywood films 7
Holy Cross Day 90
Holy Lance (relic) 23
Holy Land 16, 18, 19–41, 56–7,
     109, see also Palestine
Holy League 52
holy war 64–85, 70, 80–1
     eastern Christianity 78–9
     legal justification for 82–3,
       85
     western Christianity 64–78
Hostiensis 82
Huguenots 44
Hundred Years War
     (1337–1453) 51, 107, 134,
     135
Hungary 37, 39, 44, 132
Hussites 44, 134

I

Iberia see Spain
iconography 3
immigration 118, 124
imperialism 4, 9, 56, 140
India 138
indulgences 81, 91, 102, 105
     after the end of crusading 51,
       52
     Baltic crusades 50

crusades against heretics 43, 44, 45
  extended to non-combatants 89
  John VIII 72
  Leo IX 75
  sale of 99
  Urban II 77, 78, *see also* privileges
inheritance 96–7
Innocent III, Pope 36, 38, 88–9, 92
  Albigensian Crusade 43, 44
  church taxation 98
  on compulsory conversion 126
Innocent IV, Pope 49–50
Inquisition 44
Internet 142
Iran 59
Iraq 21, 57, 59, 61, 142–3
Isaac II, emperor of Byzantium 37
Isabella of Castile 124
Islam:
  after September 2001 139
  *jihad* 30, 61, 140, 142
  nineteenth-century triumphalism over 139–40
  religious discrimination 121
  shared religious sites with Christianity 115, *see also* Muslims
Israel 142
Israelites 67, 68, 69, 109, 134
Italy 21, 22, 57, 58, 76
  crusades against Christians in 45

eastern crusades 131
Fifth Crusade 38
French invasion of 132
popular uprisings in 42, 43
representatives in Outremer 111
Venetian Crusade 106, *see also* Venice

J

Jaffa, treaty of (1192) 34
Jakelin de Mailly 1–2, 3, 144
James I, king of Aragon 47, 122
James of Vitry 88, 89, 91, 105
Jerome 66
Jerusalem 8, 9, 12
  cosmopolitan royal court 118
  eyewitness account of massacre in 68
  Fifth Crusade 39
  First Crusade 23, 26, 77–8
  formalized map of 119
  Fourth Crusade 36
  Hospitallers in 115
  kingdom of 26, 110, 111, 113
  on medieval world maps 54
  Muslim control 57
  recovery from Muslim rule 14, 16
  Street of Palms 17
  Third Crusade 30, 34, 61, 98, *see also* Palestine
Jews 3, 7, 8, 50–1
  attacks on 105–6
  massacre of English 8, 32
  in the Old Testament 67
  Outremer 116

Rhineland pogroms 13, 22, 29, 50, 78
*jihad* 30, 61, 140, 142
Joan of Arc 132
John, king of England 102
John I Tzimisces 79
John of Brienne, king of Jerusalem 39
John of Capistrano 52
John of Joinville 100
John of Würzburg 120
John Paul II, Pope 3, 7
John VIII, Pope 72
Judas Maccabeus 135
Julius II, Pope 45
just war theory 68–70, 81, 82, 109

# K

Khwarazmian raiders 39
Knights of Dobrin 128
Kurds 30, 61, 143

# L

La Monte, J. 7
Ladislas, king of Hungary 132
Lake Peipus, battle of (1242) 129
landowners 102
Languedoc, France 43–4
Latin Mass 88, 90–1
law:
    and holy war 82–3, 85
    infringement of privileges 104
    religious discrimination 116
leadership 93–4

legacies 99
Lent 90
Leo IV, Pope 72
Leo IX, Pope 75
lepers 115
Lessing, Carl Friedrich 11
Lisbon 29, 83
literature 7
Lithuania 50, 52, 126, 128
Livonia 47, 50, 53, 101, 109, 111, 126, 127, 128
    Military Orders ruling 113, 125, 130
Lombardy 21, 22
London 8, 131
Lorraine 22
Louis IX, king of France 88
    anti-Semitism 50
    attacking Damietta 132, 133
    canonization 131–2
    crusade to Egypt 18, 40–1, 43
    embarkation site 7
    funding for crusade 96, 98, 100
    penance 105
Louis VII, king of France 27, 29, 89, 92, 94, 98
Louis VIII, king of France 44
Louis X, king of France 122
Low Countries 21, 44
Lower Weser 44
Lutheranism 50

# M

Maccabbees 67, 134, 142
Magna Carta 102
Magyars 72

Mahdia, Tunisia 77
Malik Shah, sultan of Baghdad 21, 59
Mallorca 122
Malta 52
Mamluks 40, 51, 53, 59, 60, 61–3
Mansourah, battle of (1250) 40
Manzikert, battle of (1071) 21, 59
Marienburg, Prussia 8
Markward of Anweiler 43
Martin, Abbot of Pairis 89
martyrdom 2, 16
Mayer, H. E. 62
Mecklenberg, dukes of 126
medievalism 138
mercenaries 21, 30, 80, *see also* Mamluks
Messina, Sicily 32
Michaud, Joseph François 139–40
military aristocracy 19
Military Orders 100–1, 111, 113
  Iberian 101, 122
  St John (Hospitallers) 8, 52, 101, 115, 120
  Sword Brothers 47, 49, 128
  Templars 1, 94, 101, 120
  Teutonic Knights 8, 47, 49–50, 101, 129
miracles 23, 91
Moguls 138
monasticism 70, 72–3, 74, 77, 89
Mongols 40, 61, 62, 63
Moors 29, 121–2, 124, 132
Mosul, Syria 23, 27, 61

Murcia 122
Muret, battle of (1213) 44, 124
Muslims 72
  in the Holy Land 19–41
  impact of crusades on 53–63
  *jihad* 30, 60, 79–80, 140, 142
  in Outremer 113, 115–16
  in Spain 21, 45–7, 48, 58, *see also* Islam

## N

Nablus, Palestine 117
Napoleon, Emperor of France 52, 138
nationalism 134
NATO 139
Las Navas de Tolosa, battle of (1212) 45, 124
neo-chivalry 138
neo-medievalism 4
Netherlands 44
Nevsky, Alexander 130
New Testament 64, 65, 66, 68, 76
Nicaea, Anatolia:
  battle of (1097) 23
  Seljuk capital at 59
Nicene Creed 66
Nicholas of Cologne 42
Nicopolis, battle of (1396) 51
Normandy 21, 22
Normans 73, 75
North Africa 53, 57
Norway 26
Novgorod, Russia 47
Nur al-Din, ruler of Aleppo 30, 61

# O

oath of fealty 23
Old Testament 66–7, 69, 71,
   109, 134
Orientalism 138
Origen of Alexandria 66
Orthodox Church 19
Oswald, king of Northumbria
   71
Ottoman Turks 41, 80, 136,
   140
   capture of Constantinople 52
   defeat of Mamluk Empire 62
   demise of power after Great
      War 142
   in eighteenth century 137
   western crusade armies
      crushed by 51
Outremer (Crusader states)
   26, 28, 30, 53, 110–21
   castles of 112, 113, 114
   inter-communal relations in
      117
   Jews in 51
   new sacred landscape 120
   in thirteenth century 40–1
   Turkish invasion of 121, see
      also Jerusalem

# P

pacifism 68, 70
paganism 69, 71, 74, 126–8
Palestine 1, 3, 16, 21, 26, 56,
   110, 134
   Ayyubids 53
   crusades impact on 57
   invaded by Byzantine
      Empire 79

Mamluks 62
Seljuk Turks 59
thirteenth century 41, see
   also Jerusalem
papacy 3, 7, 10, 12, 21, 74
   Baltic crusades 127, 129
   Italian crusades 45
   Second Crusade 27
   use of violence 74–6, see also
      individual popes
papal bulls 27, 38, 43, 89
Paris, Matthew 31
Paris, treaty of (1229) 44
Patarines 75
patria (homeland) 109, 134
patron saints 81–2, 122, 123
patronage 115
Peasants' Crusade (1096) 18,
   22, 93
Pelagius, Cardinal Legate 39,
   94
penance 14, 17, 70, 73, 76, 105
penitential seasons 90–1, 92
Peter I, king of Aragon 44
Peter I, king of Cyprus 51
Peter II, king of Aragon 124
Peter the Hermit 22, 93
Philip II, king of France 32, 92,
   96, 98
Philip II, king of Spain 124,
   134
pigs 117
pilgrimage 9, 15, 16, 17, 22, 74
   armed 77–8
   catering trade for 120
   following First Crusade 26
   penitential 77
   Treaty of Jaffa 34
pirates 58

Pisa 77, 131
place-names 8
Poland 50, 130, 132
Pomerania 47
portents 91
Portugal 29, 125
Prawer, Joshua 120
preaching 86–92, 107
price increases 103
privileges 14, 16, 27, 38, 81, 90, 102, 104, 127, 128, *see also* indulgences
propaganda 2, 64, 72, 109, 125, 134, 142, 143
Protestantism 44, 132, 136–7
Provence 21, 22
Prussia 47, 49, 53, 101, 109, 111, 128, 129, 130
    Military Orders ruling 113, 125

Q

Qalawun, sultan of Egypt 41
*Quantum praedecessores* (papal bull) 94
*Quia Maior* (papal bull) 38, 43, 89, 94

R

racism 9, 10, 83, 85, 115–17
ransom 98
Raymond II, Count of Toulouse 116
Raymond IV, Count of Toulouse 22
recruitment 88, 93, 101–2
    crusade sermons 88–9, 92

Fifth Crusade 38–9
First Crusade 21–2
Fourth Crusade 36
Military Orders 100–1
professionalisation of 34, 36
Second Crusade 27, 29, 65
Third Crusade 30
redemption 76, 99, 100, 102, 103
Reformation 44, 132, 136–7
relics 76, 120, 125, 131
    from Constantinople 106
    Holy Lance 23
    True Cross 31, 90
religious discrimination 115–16, 117, 121
religious persecution 8, 10, 13, 22, 29, 32, 50, 78
religious revivalism 21
Resurrection 14
Revelation of St John 68
Rhineland 13, 21, 22
    Children's Crusade 42
    Jewish pogroms in 13, 22, 29, 50, 78
Rhodes 52
Richard I, king of England 3, 4, 5, 32–4, 55, 94, 96, 104
Richard of Cornwall 100, 103
Riga 128–9
righteousness 69
Robert, Duke of Normandy 98
Robert of Rheims 33
Roderigo Diaz ('El Cid') 58
Roger II, king of Sicily 29, 43
Roman Catholicism 3, 7, 136–7
Roman Empire 57, 65, 68–9, 71, 72
Romanticism 7, 11, 138

Rome 77
Rudolph (monk) 29
Rum (Asia Minor) 23
Runciman, Steven 10, 62, 139
Russia 47, 129–30

S

Saddam Hussein 142–3
St Benedict 72–3
St James the Great 81–2, 122,
    123, 125
St John, Military Order of 8,
    52, 101, 115, 120
St Matthew, Gospel According
    to 64
St Nicholas Church, Travant 17
St Paul, Epistles of 65, 66
saints 73, 76–7, 81–2, 122, 123,
    131–2
Saladin 118
    battle of Hattin 6, 30, 31, 98
    Damascus statue of 3, 6
    and Saddam Hussein 142,
        143
    Third Crusade 61
    Treaty of Jaffa 34
    western image of 5
Saladin tithe 98
salvation 2, 16, 19, 72, 76
Samuel, Book of 67
Santiago, cult of 125, see also St
    James the Great
Sanudo, Marino 100
Saxo Grammaticus 81
Saxons 72
schismatics 43–4
Scotland 135
Scott, Sir Walter 7

sea transport 96, 99, 103
Sebastian, king of Portugal 125
Second Crusade (1145–9) 16,
    18, 26–30, 47, 65, 93, 94,
    105, 127
Second World War (1939–45)
    139
Segovia church council (1166)
    45
Seljuk empire 32, 59, 80
Serbs 51
serfs 93
sermons 86–92
Seville, capture of (1248) 47,
    122
Shepherds' Crusade (1251) 18,
    43, 102
Shia Muslims 59
Shirkuh (Kurdish commander)
    30
Sicily 21, 29, 32, 57, 75, 96
Sigurd, king of Norway 26
Simon de Montfort 44, 83,
    105, 124
Sixth Crusade (1228–9) 18
slavery 115, 117, 118
Slavs 29, 79, 126, 127, 130
sociology 10
Spain 26, 29, 109, 111
    Almohad invasion of 45, 124
    Jews in 51
    Military Orders 101, 122
    mujahiddin 80
    Muslims in 21, 45–7, 52
    racism 83
    Reconquista 45–7, 56, 81–2,
        121–5, 132
    taifa kings in 58
Stephen of Cloyes 42

Stettin 126
Sunni Muslims 58, 59
Sweden 47, 56, 127
Sword Brothers, Military
    Order of 47, 49, 128
Sybill, queen of Jerusalem 30
Syria 1, 3, 6, 16, 21, 23, 36, 39,
    55, 56, 59, 109, 110
  Ayyubids 53
  crusades impact on 57
  cultural differences 116
  invaded by Byzantine
    Empire 58, 79
  Mamluks 62
  Mongol invasion of 40
  Seljuk empire in 59
  thirteenth century 41
  unification of 30, 61

T

Tancred of Sicily 96
Tarragona, Spain 77, 131
taxation 30, 36, 38, 45, 51, 96,
    97-8, 103, 116
television 7
Templars 1, 94, 101, 120
Temple, London 8, 35
Temple Mount (Haram al-
    Sharif), Jerusalem 39
terrorism 8
Teutonic Knights 8, 47, 49-50,
    101, 129
Theobald of Champagne 103
Third Crusade (1188-92)
    30-6, 47, 56, 61, 83, 90,
    93, 94, 96, 100
Third Reich 130
Thirty Years' War (1239-68) 45

Toledo 58, 121
Tortosa, siege of (1147) 29
tourism 138
trade 103-4, 106, 111
Tripoli (principality) 26, 31, 41,
    116
Truces of God 75
True Cross (relic) 31, 90
Tunisia 18, 41, 77
Turks 2, 21, 22, 23, 27, 39, 51,
    62
  Anatolia 32
  Asia Minor 29
  invasion of Outremer 121
  Ottoman 41, 51, 52, 62, 80,
    136, 137, 140, 142
  Seljuk 32, 59, 80
Tyre, port of 31, 106, 117

U

Ugolino, Cardinal of Ostia
    99
Urban II, Pope 64, 76
  and Christian political
    history 57
  First Crusade 12-14, 16, 26
  preaching tour for First
    Crusade 21, 50, 77-8,
    89
  and Raymond of Toulouse
    22
  rebuilding of Tarragona 131

V

Valencia, Spain 47, 58, 122
Varna, battle of (1444) 51
Venetian Crusade (1122-5) 106

Venice 54–5, 62, 100, 131
   Fourth Crusade 36–8, 96, *see also* Italy
Venice, doge of 26, 37
Vikings 72, 73
violence:
   Christian distinction 73
   legal justification for 82–3, 85
   and piety 78
Virgin Mary 76, 124, 129
visions 23
vow redemptions 99, 100, 102, 103
vows 16, 81
Vulgate 66

# W

Walter Sans Avoir 22
war, justification for 68–70, 81, 82, 109
war commodities 103

Wars of Religion 44, 132
Wars of the Sicilian Vespers (1282–1302) 45, 47
Wends 125, 127
Wilhelm II, Kaiser of Germany 141
William II, king of Sicily 30
William II Rufus, king of England 21, 98
William of Tyre 120
William the Conqueror 8, 73

# Y

York, massacre of Jews (1190) 8, 32

# Z

Zara, battle of (1202) 37, 94
Zengi, ruler of Mosul and Aleppo 27, 30, 59
Zengids 80